D0995169

THE
rite STUFF

THE
rite STUFF

RITUAL IN CONTEMPORARY CHRISTIAN WORSHIP AND MISSION

edited by
PETE WARD

Text copyright © BRF 2004

Published by
The Bible Reading Fellowship
First Floor, Elsfield Hall
15–17 Elsfield Way, Oxford OX2 8FG

ISBN 1 84101 227 0

First published 2004
10 9 8 7 6 5 4 3 2 1 0
All rights reserved

Acknowledgments
Unless otherwise stated, scripture quotations are taken from
The New Revised Standard Version of the Bible, Anglicized Edition,
copyright © 1989, 1995 by the Division of Christian Education of
the National Council of the Churches of Christ in the USA, and are
used by permission. All rights reserved.

Scripture quotations marked (CEV) are from the Contemporary
English Version published by The Bible Societies/HarperCollins
Publishers, copyright © 1991, 1992, 1995 American Bible Society.

A catalogue record for this book is available from the British Library

Printed and bound in Finland

CONTENTS

CONTRIBUTORS

Pete Ward is a lecturer in Youth Ministry and Theological Education at King's College London. He is the author of numerous books on youth ministry and new forms of church including, *Liquid Church* (Paternoster, 2002) and he is also the editor of *Mass Culture* (BRF, 1999).

Jeremy Fletcher is a priest in the Church of England. He has worked in parishes in Hartlepool, Nottingham and Sutton-in-Ashfield, and has been Chaplain to the Bishop of Southwell. He is now Canon Precentor of York Minster, responsible for the planning and conduct of worship there. He is a member of the Liturgical Commission of the Church of England, but would rather be playing bass guitar and watching Bradford City return to the Premiership.

Maggi Dawn started her career as a professional musician (guitar and bass) and singer, working extensively in the field of contemporary religious music, writing new music for Christian festivals, cathedral and church liturgies and alternative worship projects. She was featured regularly on programmes by BBC Religion and Anglia TV, and released four albums of songs. In 1993 she trained for the priesthood in Cambridge, where she read for a PhD in theology and literature. After a curacy in the Ely diocese, she returned to Cambridge as Chaplain to King's College. Since September 2003 she has been the Chaplain at Robinson College, Cambridge, from where she continues to teach, write and broadcast on the theology and practice of contemporary liturgy. Maggi lives in west Cambridge with her husband and son.

Dr Anthony G. Reddie is Research Fellow at The Queens Foundation for Ecumenical Theological Education and Research Consultant in Christian Education and Development.

Ana Draper is a counsellor, and in the last few years has been training and practising in the specific field of systemic psychotherapy. She has also, for the last ten years, been actively engaged in dreaming up new ways of worshipping God that connect more effectively with contemporary culture. The aim of her chapter is to explore the different ways in which these two 'worlds' can shape and inform each other, producing a dynamic fusion of creative new ideas; not a blueprint for worship, but new possibilities within local communities. She believes that the new ideas infiltrating psychotherapy, a handful of which are explained in this book, could be helpfully applied to new thinking in the church, in what is being called the 'decade of experimentation'.

Mike Riddell is a Catholic novelist, playwright and screenwriter based in the deep south of New Zealand. He has a PhD in theology from Otago University where he teaches occasionally, while devoting most of his time to more creative pursuits. Mike has published extensively on Christian spirituality and worship, and for some years was a monthly columnist for *Third Way* magazine, but these days is mostly to be found writing for the big screen.

Jonny Baker is the National Youth Co-ordinator in the UK for the Church Mission Society. In practice this means developing and supporting mission and new ways of being church in the emerging culture among 16 to 25-year-olds. He has been involved in youth ministry for 15 years (most of those working for Youth For Christ). He is co-author of the book *Alternative Worship*, a member of *Grace*, an alternative worship community in West London and part of the wider alternative worship movement in the UK. He has co-ordinated the worship at Greenbelt Arts Festival for several years, which has been a key space in the UK for creative/ alternative/new forms of worship. He is involved in various creative projects, the most successful of which has been the Labyrinth, which he helped to design, first installed in St Paul's Cathedral, London, in 2000.

INTRODUCTION

Pete Ward

'Ritual murder, ritual child sex abuse, empty ritual, satanic ritual...' I was trying out a word association exercise on myself. Starting with the word 'ritual', I tried to find the next words that came into mind. It wasn't looking good, not very positive at all—in fact, pretty negative. Ritual clearly has a sinister or 'dark' side to it (well, it has if the way my mind works is anything to go by).

My strongest associated word, however, was 'empty'. I had grown up with the impression that formal religion was something dead and void of meaning. I remember, when I was around ten, I was, for a brief time, a choirboy at the local Anglican church. Sitting in the choir stalls, I would stare out at the congregation. 'They can't really believe this,' I thought. At least, it didn't look as if they believed it. From where I was sitting, the whole congregation looked dead. If I had had the word for it, I would have identified what was happening as 'ritual'—instead I just called it church. But I suppose this is where I got the impression that formal worship in church was empty, boring and meaningless.

A few years later, the people in the pews were much the same, but I had changed. Charismatic renewal had hit my home town and I had tasted of its joys. Suddenly the formality of the local church became a frustration and an offence. I wanted to see things freed up; I wanted to throw off the liturgy, change the music and most of all get rid of the choir. In its place we would lead Fisherfolk songs on our guitars, and hopefully someone would speak in tongues, and if we were really lucky someone else would say what it meant! Of course, I now realize that we were simply replacing one form of ritual with another; but to our mind this new way of worship was far from empty—it was full of the Spirit. This was not meaningless or routine; it was the stuff of life, charged with God. Nevertheless, it too was a highly ritualized environment, even if we were unable to recognize the fact at the time. And this is a curious fact with ritual: the more useful and meaningful it is, the less 'obvious' it is. When ritual is really powerful, it is ingrained into our social and psychological life.

A while back I asked some of my students at King's College to describe, in as much detail as they could, the start of a European Cup soccer match as it is shown on the telly. One or two were clueless, having never watched a game, but others could lead us through the exact sequence of events from when we see the two teams in the tunnel to when they eventually kick off the match. I then asked the group to describe to me, again in as much detail as possible, what happens when they visit a friend's house for supper. They were to start from when they rang the doorbell to when they began the meal. What emerged from these two descriptions was the realization that both situations were highly ritualistic. As we talked, it became clear that each was made up of a series of symbolic actions and behaviours and that, to a greater or lesser extent, we could predict what these actions would look like. In the case of the dinner party, some of us admitted that we found such moments of greeting rather 'awkward'— what kind of wine to buy, when to hand it over, to hug or not to hug, one kiss or two. It's a minefield of convention and what can only be described as routinized behaviour.

It became clear that these were both moments of greeting and that they were not isolated ritualistic moments. Human interaction is full of ritual and yet, for the most part, we remain unaware of this aspect of life. Ritual carries us through awkward moments such as the intimacy of crossing the threshold into someone's home; or moving, without violence or loss of nerve, into a highly charged sporting event. We use ritual to help us in the transition from one mode of being into another.

The power and effect of ritual can be quite overwhelming and un-expected. When Tess and I got married, we, like many other couples, were sceptical of the importance of this ritual. That is not to say that we didn't invest a great deal of time and energy in putting together a really good service and a nice 'do' to follow the church bit. It was clearly a big day for us, but 'getting married' seemed somewhat removed from helping my dad get a barrel of beer into the church hall (and then hiding it from the vicar). We loved each other and we knew that we wanted to spend the rest of our lives together and, so as far as we were concerned, we were simply celebrating this fact with our friends. Looking back on the day and talking it over, we have both realized that we were very wrong. The wedding day changed us profoundly. It changed how we saw ourselves, it changed how we saw each other, it changed how we were viewed by our families, friends and by the church fellowship, and it changed how we related to those groups. In short, the ritual moved us from one place to another: it transformed us. We were one thing before it started and something else by the time it had come to an end.

Ritual is clearly alive and well in daily life, but it is also having something of a revival in church. Some Christians are starting to explore ways of prayer and worship from what are seen as more ancient traditions —hence the rise in Celtic spirituality, Ignatian retreats and praying with icons. This book is a follow-up to an earlier volume, *Mass Culture* (BRF, 1999). *Mass Culture* looked at the communion service and its continued significance for worship and mission in contemporary culture. The mix of mission, worship and the examination and exploration of issues of culture generally referred to as 'postmodern' is continued in this volume. In *The Rite Stuff* each chapter explores a different aspect of ritual and faith. The range of these discussions is quite wide, but the unifying factor is the growing appreciation of the significance of ritual for worship and spirituality in postmodernity. In the 1970s, ritual may have been seen as empty, and religion was a dirty word. Now there is a growing appreciation of the way that formality, convention and routine in worship can facilitate an encounter with God. Ritual helps us to make a transition from the ordinary to the transcendent and back again. This is just as much the case for liturgical forms of worship as it is for charismatic or informal worship.

FINDING THE RITE STUFF

The complex nature of ritual, and its place in contemporary life and spirituality, will be the subject of the rest of this book. Anthony Reddie explores the role of ritual and symbol in the popular culture of Black people in Britain. He argues that mission and worship must take these ritualistic elements as the starting point for a contextualization of the faith that crosses the boundaries between a ghettoized church and the ebb and flow of life. An example of how these connections might take place can be found in the Labyrinth, which is currently making a tour around cathedrals in Britain (a version of which is on sale in the US, where it is called the Prayer Path). Ana Draper was one of the creators of the Labyrinth and in particular she worked on the meditations and prayers which, in my opinion, give the experience much of its spiritual depth. Her chapter in this book explores how psychology and spirituality can come together in contemporary ritual. She links the rituals from the world of therapy with those in Christian worship.

In a time of great creativity and innovation, it is important to realize that postmodern eclecticism comes at a cost. We do a deep disservice to worship and ritual if we dislocate them from their context. The context of the tradition of the church is extremely important. It is possible to get something badly wrong. An example of this can be seen in the way that some people misunderstand icons as praying to an image, rather than through an image to Christ. Maggi Dawn makes this point very powerfully when she argues that rituals should be understood as part of a symbolic system or 'rite'. Innovation is possible but the first priority must be given to respecting and understanding the integrity of the rite. Jeremy Fletcher, as a member of the Church of England Liturgical Commission, is uniquely placed to discuss the shape and purpose of liturgical 'rites'. Jeremy discusses the way that *Common Worship* has focused on the shape of ritual rather than upon the repetition of a particular form of words. With Mike Riddell, we return to the link between ritual and psychology. He argues that ritual connects us to what he calls the 'deep currents of the heart'. Through psychological archetypes, we are moved and stirred deeply by rituals and worship. These passionate insights might be set against the order of agreed rites. Jonny Baker, however, introduces Ritual Studies from anthropology as a means to understand these various frameworks.

The variety of perspectives and approaches to ritual and worship in this book indicate that ritual is far from empty. In fact, it is full—full of meaning. If the church is to have a place in people's lives, then it needs to address itself much more seriously to the question of ritual and its relationship to contemporary culture. *Mass Culture* was widely welcomed because it made this link between mission culture and worship. *The Rite Stuff* is an attempt to continue this discussion.

TEXT, AUTHORITY AND RITUAL IN THE CHURCH OF ENGLAND

Jeremy Fletcher

If any denomination could be said to have a handle on 'ritual', that denomination would be the Church of England. It doesn't take much cynical thinking to come up with pictures of a form of worship involving the repetition of set words and the performance of complex actions, set in a sacred space full of symbolic and religious significance. It is a criticism often levelled against cathedrals, for instance, that such buildings, in their Gothic finery and with their priceless objects and elaborate ceremonial, are a long way from the poor carpenter of Nazareth and the simple worship of the early Church.

RITUAL IS NOT A DIRTY WORD

It is worth remembering, though, that religious ritual is a more complicated matter than a caricature of dead ceremonies and antiquated language. Taking the word in its broadest sense, it is clear that humans have always been ritual beings: anything that is performed on a regular basis and performed according to accepted rules is a ritual. Human societies have many different rituals which in some way define that society, especially to outsiders. Ritual behaviour is almost always corporate, and even that which is performed by individuals becomes a ritual when it is done in the same way and for the same purposes as by other individuals in the same society.[1]

Many human rituals are performed for specifically religious purposes. Religious rituals have classically been divided into three types:

- those that try to control a deity for human ends, or *magic*
- those that try to ward off a deity, or *taboo*

- those that try to establish a relationship with a deity for ultimate benefit, or *communion*

This last type is most obviously a feature of Christian ritual, and in this sense it is impossible for Christians not to be ritualistic. Whenever Christians get together to celebrate their faith, they are being ritualistic. It is unfortunate that the word 'ritual' has come to have a negative connotation in some Christian circles. The Reformation rebellion against 'vain ceremonies' was against their misuse, not against religious practice in itself.

The essentials of religious ritual are actions that are repeated, corporate, agreed by the participants and the wider community, and designed for communion with God.

Many religious rituals see themselves as actually having been instituted by God. Whenever Christians gather together to break bread and drink wine, they perform a ritual whose purpose is to enable communion not just with each other but with God himself, and they do so not because it is a good idea but because God told them to do it. It does not matter whether the celebration is low-key and informal or highbrow and full of ceremony: wherever Christians gather to hear the word, share fellowship, offer worship and break bread, and do so using forms agreed by the worshipping assembly (even if they are all songs written that week by the worship band), then they are being ritualistic.

RITUAL AND THE EVERYDAY

Another feature of religious rituals is that they often have everyday actions at their heart. Frank Senn describes the basis of Christian ritual as 'bath, book, meal'.[2] Baptism, communion and hearing the word of God all begin with a 'natural' meaning. The water of baptism is the water that brings us life and makes us clean. The bread and wine of communion are the bread and wine that keep us alive. The words of scripture are the words we use to communicate and which enable us to be social beings. Religious ritual connects the secular with the sacred, the everyday with the eternal, the ordinary with the supernatural. At the heart of the Christian faith is the belief that in the life of Jesus Christ, God shares our humanity, and that through the incarnation there is nothing that cannot be redeemed: in St Augustine's terms, there is 'nothing which is not holy'.

Many religious rituals have taken what is familiar and essential, and use it to draw a community together and look beyond the immediate to the God who is behind and in it all. Indeed, such rituals are, in many ways, the only way in which the power and majesty of Almighty God can be made real to us without wiping us out. As Frank Senn says, 'rituals serve to structure a reality that would otherwise threaten to overwhelm us'.[3] How else would we 'die to sin' except through the ritual of baptism; how else be 'washed in the blood of Christ' except in the breaking of bread; how else 'hear the word of the Lord' except through scripture both read and preached? Unlike the veil in the temple, designed to keep us out of the holy of holies, such rituals usher us in, enabling us to see God face to face without being consumed.

RITUALS FOR SPECIAL OCCASIONS

Some rituals are formed to be associated with once-in-a-lifetime events such as birth, becoming an adult, marriage and death. Anthropologists define these rituals as 'rites of passage'.[4] Christian versions of these rites of passage are not hard to find, and often relate closely to similar rituals in other societies. Birth is marked with baptism in some denominations, or dedication in others. Growth to adulthood is handled less clearly, but can be baptism or confirmation (which is safer than having to kill a lion, at least, as happened in some tribal cultures). There are Christian marriage rites that have echoes of more complex ancient betrothal and joining ceremonies; and it is unsurprising that a faith which has much to say about death not being an end, but the gateway to new life, has developed a range of rituals around dying and death itself.

RITUAL WORDS AND RITUAL ACTIONS

Wherever Christians gather to celebrate the basis of their believing, and whenever they offer themselves to God at the change and crisis points of their lives, they will encapsulate the moment with some kind of mixture of words and action—what is technically called a 'rite'. Some such rites have become so encrusted with ceremonial additions that they have become almost unrecognizable from their origin, and it will always be the business of the church to scrape away the encrustations to find the most appropriate way to gather together, celebrate the faith, create a community and proclaim the good news. Because the central rituals of 'bath, book and meal' are based on symbols with a universal and timeless application, it will be the church's task to reinterpret them, not to reinvent them in every generation. Similarly, the great life events are common to all, and need rituals that are able to reinterpret them in Christian terms for the contemporary world.

These 'classic' rituals of faith and life are what the traditional denominations have as 'givens' in their ministry. Such denominations find it most difficult to reinterpret them, especially when the rituals have an ancient form that is valued for its own sake. It is almost impossible to come up with contemporary rites that take today's world as their starting point when the 'ancient' rites are so much a part of our identity. Newer churches find it easier to invent new rituals, some of which may be more temporal and of relevance only for a period, but they have the opposite problem with making rituals that carry the weight and depth of the ages. As an Anglican minister, I have often officiated, in my own centuries-old church, at the weddings of 'house church' friends, for example.

MAKING RITUALS FOR THE 21ST CENTURY IN A CENTURIES-OLD CHURCH

It is a well-known fact in Church of England circles that once you have done something three times, you've always done it—and that if you try to change it the fourth time round, someone will resign from the church council. This actually expresses one of the great truths about ritual expression: because it is repetitive, it is conservative by its very nature. Even leaders of vibrant worship conferences populated by worshippers desperate for the new things that God is doing today find themselves inundated by complaints if they change the conference format the next year, for example.

How, then, does an established and innately conservative denomination such as the Church of England handle the question of ritual? Are its agreed forms of worship trapped in such an antiquated version of religion that they are incapable of reaching the contemporary world? I believe that the answer is 'no', but because the inherent nature of religious expression is to be conservative, it may often seem as if what is happening 'in church' is not where 'the world' is at. The Salvation Army's use of brass instruments and military rank may have been cutting-edge in the Nottingham of William Booth's day, but it has a strange aura of otherworldliness today, however magnificent the contemporary ministry of the organization in the hard places of the world.

Perhaps the greatest strength of a centuries-old denomination is its very timelessness. What has survived for four and a half centuries in its Anglican form has probably survived because, at its heart, it still has religious power—because God can still be found in it. And the Church of England is one church among many whose central rituals are based on the basic needs of humanity—bath, book and meal—and on the central acts of the Christian community—baptism and communion.

SUNDAY BY SUNDAY—RITUAL AND WORSHIPPING LIFE

The Church of England has just spent several years of its life rewriting its ritual. The result, *Common Worship*, is a series of services too numerous for one book, so broadly based as to encompass a great variety of religious practice, and so flexible as to allow almost any worshipping community to express itself within the classic boundaries of belief and practice. The main contemporary communion service, for example, includes only two sentences that must always be said without alternative. Everything else is either optional or has an alternative version available. This is a reflection of the fact that 'on the ground', different worshipping communities have their own ways of doing things, and as long as the essentials are there, the specifics may vary from place to place. It is therefore up to each parish or community to work out its own ritual practice: there is no one 'set' form.

This is a marked difference from a century ago. Though the Church of England has never been a uniform organization, attempts were made to prevent overtly ritualistic practices (such as genuflection, elaborate robes, making the sign of the cross and so on), to the extent that some clergy and even one bishop were put on trial in the courts, and some were imprisoned as a result. In the ensuing years, as this kind of ceremonial became more accepted, manuals were written that tried to formalize such ritual actions excessively. Books such as *The Ritual Reason Why* and *The Parson's Handbook* gave detailed instructions on every aspect of ceremonial in church, down to the exact way to fold the linen and which hand to hold the cup with.

The common factor behind both these approaches to ritual (either preventing certain things or prescribing exactly how they should be performed) is that there is assumed to be a 'right' way to do things, and that getting it 'wrong' would in some way invalidate what was done. Some centuries earlier, a Roman Catholic priest called Martin Luther used to suffer agonies if he made a mistake in saying the Mass, partly because he believed that doing so would call the whole thing into question. But there is a difference between doing things 'ritualistically' and providing a ritual that takes a basic life event and a central point of Christian belief and becomes charged with the glory of God. In its deliberations over its worship in the last years of the 20th century, the Church of England recognized that all it could do centrally was to provide words that were doctrinally sound and full of the depth and breadth of faith. The Liturgical Commission and General Synod have provided a *rite*, but the enacting of the rite—the making of a *ritual*—is a matter for the local church.

STRUCTURE, NOT TEXT

The central services are there, of course. Bath, book and meal are provided in a variety of ways: four 'orders' for communion; different types of initiation services; and a basic structure of *A Service of the Word*, with some worked-out ways of doing it. What is new is a concentration on structure rather than text. The structure marks out the essentials of the ritual, and the text begins to put flesh on the bones. When there was only one way of celebrating communion, according to *The Book of Common Prayer*, the structure of the service was less obvious, because there was nothing else to compare it to. But then a ground-breaking book, *The Shape of the Liturgy*, was published just after the Second World War. In it the author, Gregory Dix, argued that communion in its original form at the last supper had a central shape—the fourfold action of Jesus taking the bread and wine, giving thanks for them, breaking the bread, and giving it to his disciples. Subsequent Church of England communion services went on to make something of this shape, designing the central part of the service around it.

This concentration on structure, fleshed out by texts, is an essential part of Anglican liturgy today. The communion service, for example, has four major sections—Gathering, Liturgy of the Word, Liturgy of the Sacrament, and Dismissal—each with their key elements. *A Service of the Word* is made up of a series of headings, and the idea is that the headings are put together to form a basic structure, which can be used for any kind of non-eucharistic service from an informal meditation to alternative worship,[5] to a family service, to Morning Prayer. It may seem logical and even commonplace now, but this is a revolution in 'official' Anglican thinking, and puts the responsibility for the design and enactment of worship firmly in the hands of local worship leaders, rather than the 'centre'. All this means that the essentials of Christian ritual are in place, and the key elements are held in common, but there is no attempt to legislate for how such acts of worship should be carried out.

If Anglican communion services look much the same in five years' time as they did 20 years ago, that will not be because the 'centre' of the Church of England requires them to be so. The opportunity is there for churches and communities to reassess exactly how they perform their central acts of worship and look carefully at how they might relate to their context and cultural setting. The structure and words of the communion service are not restrictive in the end, and it is entirely possible to create a setting in which the connection with everyday and special meals can be made, and the resonances with the great meals of the Bible and the banquet that we shall enjoy in heaven can be clearly heard. There is no requirement to 'ape' the ceremonial of previous generations, even if many of the Church of England's buildings might point us in that direction. Even with our buildings there has been change, and in the last 50 years many churches have been redesigned to bring the table closer to the people, and to bring the leader(s) of worship into the heart of the congregation, not 20 yards away from contradiction.

The problem is that, as Evelyn Underhill pointed out many years ago, once a ritual has been brought into being, it takes on a life of its own and often defies control or change. Take the way in which people receive communion, for example. Walking a long way from one's pew, up through the church, to receive bread and wine kneeling down has become an absolutely essential part of Christian worship for many people. When my own church was being redesigned ten years ago, we 'borrowed' another church down the road. It had no communion rail, and nowhere to kneel. Many people were at a loss to know why they felt so uncomfortable, and it took many months for them to get used to this new way of receiving. The essential part of communion as a ritual is the eating of bread and drinking of wine, but for many people their posture as they do this is just as important. Other parts of the ritual experience can take on equal importance: one member of my congregation found it physically impossible to sing a hymn out of the *Songs of Fellowship* book, and had to find the same words (it was 'Breathe on me, breath of God') in *Hymns Ancient and Modern* before he could join in. The book he sang it from was as important as the hymn he was singing.

The Church of England, in common with most of the established denominations, takes as its central rituals the services of communion and a 'word' service, with baptism as the key rite of initiation. It provides a clear structure for these services, provides a variety of texts and requires essential elements to be in place, but does not then prescribe how these services should be carried out. The texts are most like a drama script, but with very few stage directions. This means that parishes next door to each other will carry them out in radically different ways: one may have an elaborate procession where the Book of the Gospels is carried in procession, accompanied by the processional cross; and another may have a group of people reading from *The Dramatised Bible*. In both cases the essence of the ritual is there—a concentration on the scriptures that contain the word of life—but its expression is different and appropriate to the particular community.

RITUALS FOR LIFE

The Church of England also has a long history of dealing with 'rites of passage'. In theory every child born in England has the right to be baptized in their parish church, and in practice 25 per cent still are. Every couple wanting marriage for the first time has a similar right, and the burial service is open to all. Something like 50 per cent of all funerals in England in 2001 were conducted by Anglican ministers. In writing new rites and creating new rituals for these events, the Church of England was mindful of the need to express Christian truth for these events, while connecting with the experience, context and culture of the participants, most of whom have no regular contact with their church.

The way this was done was to look into the heart of ritual theory and take the essence of rites of passage as a starting point. This says that such rites function as a journey, during which the participant crosses a 'threshold'. The child becomes an adult, the man and woman become a couple, and, at death, the human being goes from life to death and what lies beyond. Classic rites of passage have rituals for preparation, crossing the threshold, and starting the new life. The Latin term for threshold is *limen*, so the rites for preparing are called 'preliminary'.

This view of the rite of passage as a journey has informed all the new 'pastoral' services.[6] In *The Book of Common Prayer* and *The Alternative Service Book* the only ritual provided for the time of death was the funeral service itself. Now there are rites provided for before and at the time of death, after a death, before the funeral, and after the funeral, recognizing that the mourners make their own journey. As their loved one crosses the threshold, so do they, into a new life without them. The marriage service in its traditional form always emphasized the journey made by the couple: they enter separately, meet at the step, move to the altar and leave together. The new rite makes more of this by separating the 'declarations' ('I will') from the 'vows' ('till death us do part'). The declarations used to be made at the church door, and are a throwback to the betrothal ceremony, when a couple declared their intention to marry. Perhaps there may yet be an 'engagement' rite: at least we have more prayers provided for the occasions when the couple's banns are read, which is a start.

The pastoral services make the point that the journey through a rite of passage is not made by the participants alone. 'God is with us every step of the way.'[7] These rites give assurance, then, of God's presence in the great and small events of our lives, but also provide challenges to move people along in their journey of faith. The funeral service is unapologetically Christian. When a question was asked about the possibility of providing a rite for those of questionable or no faith, the answer came that the Church of England is not in the business of providing rites for non-Christians, and anyway it should not make judgments about people that only God can make. That is not to say that these rites should take no account of the reality of people's lives. Two decades ago, the presence of the children of a couple to be married would have been unusual and embarrassing. Now it is more normal, though occasionally difficult, and there is a prayer provided that acknowledges this and prays for the new status of the whole family.

The provision of a pastoral ritual must take account of two things—the unchanging nature of God, and the changing nature of the world. All too often, the church has reflected the unchanging nature of God by remaining entirely the same while the world changes around it. These new rites hold fast to the doctrine of God, but allow this to be applied into a new cultural and demographic situation. For the ritual to 'work', it must be relevant to the participants and wholly fixed on God. Again, all that is provided by 'the centre' is the script, leaving the local minister and community to work out the details. Hints are given as to what might happen. For example, in the funeral service 'suitable symbols of the life and faith of the departed person may be placed on or near the coffin'.[8] There is ample scope for making this a real celebration of the person who has died, while not distracting from the affirmation of hope in the resurrection which is at the centre of the service.

RITUALS FOR THE 21ST CENTURY

It is entirely possible to be a Christian and remain entirely on your own, but it is better to meet with your fellow Christians and celebrate your faith. To do this, there needs to be an agreed way of meeting, and a religious ritual is born. The Church of England inhabits buildings many of which have housed these rituals for over a thousand years, and rapid adaptation to change is not the first thing that springs to its mind. This is both a strength and a weakness. It is a strength because some of the power and depth to be found when Christians worship together comes from a sense of timelessness and a concentration on things that have not changed for millennia. It is a weakness because such rituals can become ends in themselves, not connected to the rest of the lives of the participants.

The 'official' response of the Church of England has been to be less prescriptive about ritual action, and to be flexible with ritual words, concentrating on providing a structure on which a contemporary ritual can be built which still hooks in to the timeless truths of the Christian faith. This is particularly true of its pastoral services, which by their very nature must relate to the society they aim to serve. The changes made are probably too conservative, but there is ample scope for all sorts of adaptation that will help a community tread the fine line between relevance and timelessness. When people encounter a ritual performed by committed worshippers who own what they are doing and who find in it a communion with God, they do not just see a corporate activity, but begin to glimpse something of the reality of God. I would venture that this holds for the liveliest of charismatic celebrations, the most alternative of alternative worship, and the most historic Prayer Book Evensong. Much of the Church of England is at the historic end, but if it gets its ritual right, it has the opportunity to welcome many people to the life of faith.

THE ART OF LITURGY

Maggi Dawn

Christian worship: a hot topic or a worn-out debate? The soft-rock worship music associated with the charismatic revival of the 1970s and '80s has long since been accepted into mainstream worship, and a sizable industry has grown up to market the genre it created. Guitars may now be as acceptable as pipe organs, but feelings still run high as new forms of worship continue to threaten the comfortable habits of worship of the average parish church. In addition, there is a growing trend for worship groups that do not belong to the institutionalized church. The worship debate, it seems, is a perennial one.

This is in some ways unsurprising, for public worship is absolutely central to the life of any church. Sunday services are based around our main rites of worship, and attendance at these is, subconsciously, treated as a badge of belonging. A person might attend all the midweek prayer groups and business meetings of a church, but if they never attended the main service, they would, in most churches in Britain, be regarded as fringe members. Our rites of worship, then, are part of the glue that holds church life together; if these rites are failing to engage the people who participate in them, we should sit up and take notice.

It is the function of rite to create a context in which Christians can worship God within the framework of the gospel. Any assessment of rite must therefore be concerned not only with historical continuity and theological coherence, but also with the effectiveness of rite in enabling Christians to worship. We cannot afford to dismiss consistent complaints against traditional forms of worship as mere petulance or ignorance. Gregory Dix wisely pointed out that it is all too easy to become so enamoured of particular forms of rite that we forget that it is God whom we seek to worship, and not the works of our own hands.[9]

It is all too common for churches to attempt to paper over the cracks by simply adding a few items to an existing form of worship, aiming to make it 'more relevant for the young people'. I would suggest, however, that not only does this practice fail to make worship relevant, it also destroys the structure of a traditional rite, the result often being a mismatch both of style and content. Despite the trend within postmodern culture to create new forms by re-mixing material from various sources, there is no less skill involved in putting a contemporary service together than in interpreting a traditional one, and if worship of any description is to be accessible and coherent, a clear view of the form and purpose of rite remains essential. It is my firm belief that the ineffectiveness of rites of worship is wrongly blamed on their being 'traditional': the problem more often is that their form is treated as a container into which all sorts of bits and pieces can be added without any attention to the overall sense of the service. I will argue here, then, that in the development of the worship of the church, traditional rites still have much to offer but that, whether rites are contemporary or traditional, the integrity of their form is vital to their effectiveness.

RITE: WHAT HAVE WE INHERITED?

First, though, we need some definitions. The word 'rite' is used in a number of different ways, but I shall use it to refer to recognized and constantly repeated forms of Christian worship. I shall include within this liturgical and non-liturgical traditions, and such recent developments as the patterns of worship typical of the New Churches,[10] but not the more experimental or 'alternative' forms of worship. I shall refer to these as 'paraliturgical'[11] events, which act both as a critique of rite and as a forum for its development.

Liturgy

Liturgy is the kind of distilled, scripted service found in the prayer books of various denominations. A liturgy is made up of various parts, but is conceived of as a whole: the order of the component parts of the service is as important as the parts themselves, and the entire service is thought of as an act of worship. For instance, an Anglican Eucharist, or Holy Communion, begins with the threefold Christian confession of faith, praise and sin, and continues with a Collect (the prayer of the day that collects or sums up in miniature the sense of the whole service), two or more readings from scripture, the communion, and a blessing and dismissal. The order of these items is significant for the meaning of the whole: the Gospel reading must precede the eucharist, in order to symbolize the fact that the presence of Christ is made real to us in two ways—through the word and through the sacrament. You could, therefore, have a eucharist with no sermon, but you could not have it without the Gospel reading. In liturgy, then, the parts of the service and their order are important, gradually building up the meaning of the rite as a whole. Although regional and seasonal variations occur, the shape of the service is always basically the same.

Liturgy of the hours

The eucharist is only one form of liturgy. Liturgical worship grew from two distinct historical roots—the cathedral and the monastic traditions—and, despite many centuries of liturgical evolution, the tenor of public worship is still affected by these historical differences. In the cathedrals of the early centuries of Christian worship, the services reflected the communal worship of the gathered community; worshippers met and acknowledged one another as they worshipped God as a group. The eucharist still reflects this type of service—it is both public and communal. But in the monasteries of the time, another form of worship developed that became known as the Divine Office, or the Liturgy of the Hours. This was a daily sequence of seven services of readings and prayers. Every three hours, the entire community would down tools and head for chapel, where they would hear and recite a cycle of scripture readings, psalms, canticles and prayers. While this worship was 'public' in the sense that it was a gathering of people, the purpose of the Office was to aid personal devotion and discipline in prayer. So the sense or 'direction' of worship was that of each individual praying, rather than a corporate expression.

The distinction between cathedral and monastic worship has become blurred over time, but the distinction between corporate and individual prayer is worth bearing in mind, for a rite does not comfortably achieve both things at the same time. We put unrealistic expectations upon rite if we seek individual contemplation within a corporate rite, or fellowship at the Daily Office. Different kinds of service can, and should, have different purposes and expectations.

Rite of the word

Another kind of rite is known as the 'rite of the word', or 'preaching service', and although some liturgists trace its origins back to first-century synagogue worship, the classic 'hymn sandwich' associated with many Free Churches grew out of the dissenting groups of the Reformation. Convinced of the corruption of liturgy, and that the Office was beyond revision or purification, separatists practised a non-sacramental form of worship that consisted of extempore prayer, Bible reading and expository preaching. Two things are noteworthy here. The first is that the weight of this rite rests on the preaching of the word of God, whether it is expository, or instructional teaching, or 'kerygmatic'—the kind of inspirational preaching that is expected to be transformative through an encounter with God. The second is that within the preliminaries to preaching, the style of prayer tends to be instructive or intercessory rather than contemplative. The whole direction of this kind of rite, then, is instructive: it is delivered from the platform rather than drawn from the people.

Most of the churches in Britain use some variation on these forms of rite as their main services of public worship. The New Churches, which came into being out of the charismatice revival of the 1970s and '80s are often thought of as practising free-form worship rather than a 'rite', yet even they have developed a regularized pattern of worship which is a variation on the 'rite of the word' as described above. The distinguishing feature of New Church rite is its extended periods of sung worship, but the item of chief importance remains the preaching of the word. A New Church friend mentioned to me recently, 'Our sung worship is supposedly our trademark, but you can see the real priority from our weekly prayer sheet—it always requests prayers for Sunday's preacher, never for the worship leaders.'

WHAT'S WRONG WITH RITE?

Christian rite, then, varies in form and intent, but has the same basic purpose—to create a context where people can meet God in the framework of the gospel. This brief summary might suggest that there is enough variety and flexibility in Christian rite to make room for all kinds of people. But if we are in any doubt that Christian rite is failing to engage people with God in their daily lives, we need only to look at the proliferation of 'alternative', 'experimental', 'emerging' or otherwise-labelled worship events that take place both inside and outside the walls of the church. It is now common for churches to host regular, special worship events in addition to their main church services, and attendance at these often includes people who do not attend the main services at all. Similar events also take place outside the context of church altogether, organized and attended by Christians who have not lost their faith, but who no longer feel connected to the life and worship of the institutional church.[12] In both cases, these represent worship in a wide range of styles. Some reinterpret ancient traditions, while others invent new, contemporary forms of worship, many of which are 'one-offs', created specially for a single event.

It is not simply the existence of these 'extra-curricular' worship events that suggests that rite is failing: after all, there has always been a healthy 'fringe' of activities that push the boundaries of what is acceptable and normal in worship, and contribute to the development of rite. Rather it is the proliferation of such services, combined with the fact that some people attend them to the exclusion of the main rites of the church, that suggests that those rites are failing in their purpose for a significant number of worshippers. But this occurrence is not unprecedented in the history of rite. There was a similar flourishing of alternative worship activities during the baroque period (late 17th century) when liturgy was particularly inaccessible to the ordinary worshipper. The Mass was enacted solely by priests, at a great distance from the people; they felt uninvolved, and began to focus their worship in other ways. As Jungmann puts it, the worship of the people 'moved towards the periphery'.[13] Wainwright makes a similar observation, noting that whenever Christian rite became a splendidly performed but distant activity, a proliferation of 'paraliturgical activities' occurred as people sought additional and more congenial ways to express their worship.[14]

In the context of the 21st century, however, people are less bound to the institution of church, and no longer feel obliged to defer to priests or ministers in writing and leading services of worship. So the current range of 'paraliturgical activities' extends even further, to include 'unofficial' communion services, baptisms and weddings. This would seem to indicate that for a significant number of people, rite is currently failing to provide a context in which they can meet God in a way that feels authentic to them.

Authenticity, not style

The current alternatives to the rites of the church are not inspired merely by issues of style, then. In fact, it is noticeable that paraliturgical activities include not only the progressive and experimental use of contemporary forms, but also a revival of traditional Compline, 'Taizé' services, and various forms of 'Celtic' worship, which, despite mixing ancient ideas with recent constructs, appeal to a sense of history and often make use of traditional language and music. This being the case, there must be some other problem with traditional rite.

I would suggest that the problem is a clash between two different needs for authenticity. Tradition is no longer self-authenticating in our society: from government and the monarchy to marriage and the family, traditional institutions and ceremonies are questioned, and the argument that things have 'always been done this way' simply won't wash any longer. The authenticity and validity of worship cannot be assumed because of its longevity. Recent research into social attitudes suggests that people increasingly base their acceptance of institutional figures and practices on perceived authenticity, not position or qualification. Leaders no longer gain authority through title, position or qualifications, but by visibly living up to what they claim to believe, and beliefs and practices are not accepted on the basis of objectivity, but on whether it is also 'true for me'.

Christian rite, then, needs not only to be authentically Christian in terms of maintaining historical and doctrinal continuity. It also needs to allow for worshippers to express their worship in ways that seem 'real' to them. These two elements are difficult to reconcile, and the uneasy relationship between them often leads to very stilted performance of rite. Well-intentioned attempts to make worship relevant while at the same time staying faithful to the Christian tradition lead to a hotch-potch of items, with different styles and purposes. Many a parish in England will combine within their main Sunday service a traditional eucharist with a 'time of worship' led by a guitar band, a youth drama and a children's talk, often removing some elements of the eucharistic liturgy to make time for the additions. The intention is good—it's meant to provide something for everyone—but the result is often an incoherent rite, which fails to engage the majority of worshippers in any significant spiritual encounter. Rather than pleasing everyone, as often as not such services please no one.

Apparently, although rite is not 'hitting the spot' for large numbers of worshippers, existing alternatives quite readily draw from traditional sources. Observing the trends in a variety of paraliturgical activities, it is interesting to note that, either instinctively or deliberately, most groups make use of similar principles to ancient liturgy. Both 'alternative' or 'emerging' groups and more established formats, such as the worship of Taizé, formulate and follow a clear structure, are led by an individual or group, are based around some kind of theme or plan, and—most noticeably—are focused entirely on the act of worship itself: there are no notices, and where there is any group discussion it is specifically focused on the theme of the service. This suggests to me that people have not stopped wanting to participate in structured corporate worship. It is not rite itself that is the problem, but the way in which it is currently practised. Rather than throw out the baby with the bathwater, then, it would be better to ask what works well in traditional rite, that should be preserved or reinterpreted. I believe that the traditional rites of the church still have a great deal to offer us: there are texts of great literary beauty that should be preserved, structural shapes that can be reinterpreted, and liturgical principles to guide us in writing vital new rites.

Performed well, traditional rites can be every bit as imaginative and spiritually engaging as the newest and best of the alternatives. One Good Friday, for instance, I presided over a high Anglo-Catholic service of 'Ante-communion and Veneration of the Cross'. The significance of Ante-communion is that all the shape of a eucharistic service is observed, but there is no communion, signifying the absence of Christ in the feast. The incense was still heady from the previous evening, and the theatricality of the procession and prayers was on a grand scale. Towards the end of the service, as the choir sang an exquisitely poignant piece of music, a plain wooden cross, draped in very fine purple silk, was carried slowly through the congregation and placed on the altar steps. After a lengthy silence, my task was to climb the steps and pull the silk from the cross, allowing it to float to the ground. The atmosphere was electric, and I was suddenly struck not just by the spiritual meaning of the moment, but by its similarity with so much of the 'alternative' worship I have been involved in. Here in the most traditional of services were the same elements—poetry, prayer, scripture, music, symbol, silence. Just like alternative worship, the power of the service was in its shock value—the empty altar, the bare cross. And there was the same feeling that we had, unmistakably, looked into the face of God.

Tradition and innovation can be close bedfellows if we don't insist on a rigid adherence to either. But in addition, one of the great benefits of rite is highlighted by the downside of experimental worship. For by virtue of being experimental, new services require a large investment of time and effort both to produce and to participate in. Some of the more renowned 'alternative' and 'emerging' groups in the UK have discovered that the worship of any group quickly falls into a repeating pattern. One group I know of felt this indicated that they were 'losing their edge', and deliberately began to try out new ideas. But a number of other groups—notably those among which their main personnel are going through major career development or raising small children—have embraced the tendency to repeat effective patterns of worship, and have happily settled into a 'rite' of their own. In other cases, particularly where groups have not broken away from church but have put on special services of worship within the church's programme, those elements of the experimental worship that have worked well have eventually been incorporated into the regular rite of the church.

Certainly one of the benefits of rite is that it can be reproduced anywhere, anytime, by anyone, without needing excessive preparation, and the simple logistics of making regular corporate worship possible for ordinary communities suggest that a regularization of rites is necessary and desirable. But another benefit of the repeating pattern of rite is exactly its sameness. The same ritual repeated many times throughout different experiences allows for a more dynamic relationship with the rite: not only do we read the text, but it begins to read us too. Repeating patterns when you're full of energy and doing well might seem lazy or unimaginative. But rite gives us a tool of prayer that still works as it did in the early monasteries: praying through the same texts over decades, through love and celebration, through bereavement and unemployment, through lean and rich times, unlocks a deeper level of engagement with those texts, and this is a dynamic we would miss if we abandoned the repeating habit of rite.

NEW INNOVATIONS IN RITE

Old forms and new, then, should be able to exist side by side and feed each other, rather than being pitted against one another as rivals. A false dichotomy between traditional and contemporary makes us forget that services we regard as time-honoured traditions were, at their inception, often quite daring and new. Until recently, I was Chaplain of King's College, Cambridge. One of our home-grown traditions, the Festival of Nine Lessons and Carols, gives the impression of being as old as the Bible, but when it was introduced in 1918, it was quite a forward-thinking move. The chaplain, Eric Milner-White, noticed that many undergraduates returning from the war were struggling with their faith, but found the chapel liturgy inaccessible and off-putting. In response to this, he created a simple service that would tell the Christmas story in a series of readings, interspersed by carols that illustrated the story.[15] The service was a runaway success, and within a few decades had become established as a tradition. Eighty-five years later, it is broadcast annually from King's and continues to inspire millions of listeners. But the story behind the service is equally inspiring, for it illustrates the fact that even rites we consider as 'traditional' started out as innovative experiments produced to meet the need of the moment.

THE ART OF LITURGY

Rite isn't beyond hope—but we need to recover the art of constructing and performing rite in such a way that it does create the context for people to meet God. Treating rite with too much reverence, forgetting that it has a purpose beyond itself, will ossify it, but it can equally be rendered lifeless if we don't take it seriously enough. In order to work well, rite has to be treated as a whole piece, giving it an integrity akin to the integrity of a work of art. In an effort to provide 'something for everyone', many churches, despite the best of intentions, end up not with a coherent act of worship but with a mismatched variety of bits and pieces. An ad hoc adaptation of rite, rather than an improvement, gives us the worst of both worlds, placing side-by-side items that do not belong together either in terms of their liturgical direction or their style. No one would consider inserting a

Shakespearean speech into an Alan Bennett play, or an excerpt from Ian McEwan into a Jane Austen novel, and even in a decade that has done the 'edited highlights' format to death, it would be inconceivable to see a Radiohead gig advertised with a Mozart symphony as a support act. Why? Not because of a qualitative comparison, but because the mix simply doesn't make sense.

Mastering the art of rite takes years of work, but there are two ground rules that are absolutely essential to shaping a rite. The first is to identify its purpose and direction, which, as in the development of monastic and cathedral rites, will set its limits: is this rite principally a corporate act of worship or a service in which worshippers can gather for individual contemplation? A eucharist is not enhanced by 45 minutes of expository Bible teaching; a preaching service will not deliver a contemplative service full of symbolic meaning; the intensity and rhythm of daily Morning Prayer is interrupted if it is loaded down with the expectation of in-depth fellowship. The beauty and success of Taizé worship is its uninterrupted focus on individual contemplation—rather than corporate worship, there is a sense that worshippers are united in their individual quest to meet with God.

The second rule of shaping a rite is to choose limits in terms of the elements that are brought together to create the rite—language, music, choreography and the use of symbol. Choosing these with an eye to the whole, rather than as a series of separate elements, gives coherence to the rite. But setting limits for a particular rite doesn't necessarily mean conforming to expectation. For instance, liturgies that are associated with a particular style of music can be completely transformed simply by using an unexpected and unaccustomed musical setting. Ely Cathedral recently hosted a jazz Mass, in which the words and structure of the liturgy were unchanged, but the expected choral music was replaced entirely with a jazz setting. One of the striking differences between choral music and jazz is that while choral music aims for a very precisely rehearsed rendition of a piece, jazz is never the same twice. The juxtaposition of a completely familiar liturgy with the unpredictable, spontaneous nature of jazz gave a completely fresh twist to the theological meaning of the liturgy—allowing the timeless, transcendent quality of a God who never changes to be brought into a new focus as the God who is completely alive, and has the capacity to surprise us with originality and freshness.

Almost anything can be incorporated into rite. The limits are not on what is admissible, but on how much one can place within any single rite. An isolated jazz piece within a choral service would be unlikely to be effective, but a jazz mass is a complete epiphany.

Form and the creation of meaning

When rite is crafted within chosen limits, it gains focus, and not only does this vary the possible modes of worship, it also opens up a range of theological meaning. This was brought home to me through attending two completely different services, each of which took place in Holy Week. While focusing on the same idea, they were different both in form and style, but each was consistent with the choice of the direction of rite, and the cultural and musical style in which it was presented. The result was two services that gave entirely different 'takes' on the problem of a flawed and failing humanity, and the possibility of being remade through God's grace.

The first took place at King's College, Cambridge, where every year on Good Friday the service begins with Allegri's *Miserere*. This famous and beautiful setting of Psalm 51—traditionally the prayer of David after his adulterous affair with Bathsheba and its catastrophic consequences—begins with two choirs singing from opposite ends of the chapel, with the soloist between them. The desolation and isolation of sin is emphasized by the separation of the different voices. Gradually, as the music continues, the soloist and two choirs process through the thousand-strong congregation until they meet and sing the last chorus together, bringing a sense of spiritual as well as musical resolution. The *Miserere* perfectly sets the scene for a service that considers the universality and long history of the human predicament. This piece, that has been sung countless times before, and will be again, connects this particular rite to many other Good Fridays past and present. In addition, the choral tradition deliberately plays down individual identity—the identical clothing, the likeness of this performance to those of previous years, the similarity of this kind of worship to that in other chapels, cathedrals and churches, serve to produce the sense that this act of worship includes all people, at all times and in all places. This service, then, spoke of the universality of human separation from God through the whole sweep of human history.

By contrast, a few years earlier, I was involved in a service where the worship was led by Bryn Haworth, the outstanding R&B guitarist and singer-songwriter. Bryn's skill is second to none, but there is nothing transcendent about the atmosphere he creates. Even in a huge auditorium, you get the feeling that he's playing for you in your own living-room. He talked to the congregation between songs, gig-style, using his personality as well as his musical skills to create an atmosphere of worship. Then, when the audience was right in the palm of his hand, he changed the mood: the band disappeared into the shadows, and it was just him and his guitar. The people became absolutely still as he began to sing a haunting melody:

> What kind of love is this, that gave itself for me?
> He who had done no wrong, was crucified for me…
> What kind of love is this, a love I'd never known?
> I didn't even know his name—what kind of love is this?[16]

There wasn't a dry eye in the house. Again, flawed humanity met the love and mercy and forgiveness of God, but this time it was personal. One man's intensely individual act of worship drew everyone else into the realization of the individual significance of human sin and God's forgiveness. One of the criticisms sometimes levelled at an ordained priesthood is an objection to the idea that one person embodies the worship of the people. But here, in an altogether different setting, was an act of 'priestly' symbolization I have rarely seen surpassed: one man sang, and everyone met God.

CONCLUSION

Rite, then, whether ancient, modern or on the experimental edge, depends for its effectiveness not on some kind of demonstrable cultural relevance, but on its integrity of form. Rite may be boundaried by particular doctrinal and ecclesiological expectations but, like any performance that uses words, music, movement and symbol to express human belief and emotion, it needs to have artistic integrity. In other words, liturgy is not merely a repository of theology or sound doctrine, but a first cousin of the world of the arts. The best of liturgical worship already knows this; the best of the new and experimental forms of worship have rediscovered it. There's an art to rite—a gallery of different styles and eras. What counts is not how old it is, but how well we select and perform the elements.

I am fairly certain that much of what is going on at the experimental edge of worship will, sooner or later, serve to reshape the rite of the church. But while I welcome innovation, I do not believe that it should replace the best of traditional worship, but that the two should inform each other. I would suggest that the way forward is neither to replace tradition with innovation, nor to adapt traditional services by inserting extra bits in the hope of making them relevant, but to allow different forms of rite to exist side by side. In other words, let's abandon the 'variety show' approach to worship, and dare to extend our repertoire of rite, performing each within chosen limits in order to maintain an integrity of form. Our rites will then stand a better chance of fulfilling their purpose— not merely to perpetuate a tradition, but to create a context where people can engage with God.

PERSONALIZED RITUAL

Pete Ward

We are seeing a widespread return to ritual. This is not just true in national life—for example, the response to the Queen's Golden Jubilee and the Queen Mother's funeral. It is also true in churches, both in the UK and around the world. Charismatic house churches are starting to use liturgical elements in their worship. Youth congregations commonly invent 'contemporary rituals' to enrich their worship. In the wider society it is becoming more and more common for people to seek to mark significant occasions through rituals, ranging from a short memorial to mark the scattering the ashes of a loved one, to the blessing of a baby. If I think back to the weddings I have attended in the last few years, they have all been different, and this difference has come from the creative input of those most closely involved. Ritual is clearly far from dead. Yet at the same time it seems that we are not content with something off the peg—we want a more tailored look. What these new forms of ritual have in common is that they have been, to some extent, individually designed. They are 'personalized rituals'.

Personalized ritual presents significant challenges for the Christian Church. In the past, through various means of control, religious authorities have sought to limit the range of diversity in ritual practice. Now, not only is this control being significantly relaxed but the missionary nature of ministry demands new approaches. In this chapter we will look at some of the new developments in what I have called 'personalized ritual'. I draw upon a number of different contexts where ritual is used in contemporary worship, including charismatic worship, alternative worship and new forms of personalized prayer. Using these contexts and others as a background, we will explore some of the points of discussion that emerge from the tendency to develop personalized worship. I have arranged this material under three headings—'The ecstatic and the incarnational', 'The expressive and the instrumental', and 'The socially constructed and the inspired'. After these discussions, the chapter closes by looking at personalized ritual in practice. It describes a ritual in detail and then draws some reflections from the experience of making and taking part in a personalized ritual.

THE ECSTATIC AND THE INCARNATIONAL

In his book *Alternative Worship and the Church of England*, Paul Roberts makes a distinction between charismatic worship, which he calls ecstatic, and alternative worship, which he says is incarnational.[17] This distinction is very interesting. Roberts' point is that alternative worship groups place a significant emphasis upon the creation of a worship event. Working together in groups, they plan and then run their worship events and services. It is through this shared activity, and most especially through the things that they create, that they encounter God. Roberts sees this as 'incarnational' because the experience of God is mediated through cultural events and artefacts: God is seen in things.

What Roberts calls 'incarnational' worship, a Catholic theologian such as Leonardo Boff might see as 'sacramental'.[18] Boff's treatment of sacrament allows him to view a variety of objects as the means of God's revelation. Curiously, for Boff, this sacramental theology is also highly personalized. Thus he argues that these everyday sacramental objects, for him, include an old cup tied to the kitchen sink and his father's last half-smoked cigarette. Boff treats these symbolic objects as a means of encounter with God, and thus they are, in his terms, everyday sacraments.

This incarnational or sacramental approach to worship is contrasted by Roberts to more 'ecstatic' worship. He does not elaborate on what this kind of spirituality may entail, but he links it to charismatic worship. Reading between the lines, it would seem that what he has in mind is some kind of interior experience of God. It is ecstatic perhaps because it does not just take the individual out of themselves but in some ways they are also transported out of this world. Thus, to simplify perhaps a little, incarnational worship looks for God in the things of this world, while ecstatic worship seeks an encounter that takes us beyond ourselves.

Such a distinction, even if it is only implied, must be challenged. The ritual of worship cannot be so prescribed. So-called incarnational worship, at its best, delivers an encounter with God, and there is no reason to assume that this might not be, to some extent, ecstatic. Spiritual ecstasy is perfectly possible within the process of a worship that has been constructed by a group, or in worship that values 'things'. Arguably, if we remain located in the things of worship rather than connecting to what these things represent, then we have failed. Similarly, it must be a false notion to see charismatic or Pentecostal worship as simply an internalized form of escapism. The personalized experience of God in charismatic worship is mediated not only by songs but also by the other people involved. This means that there is an expectation that Christ will be communicated through the worship of those who gather together. In this sense, charismatic worship is every bit as incarnational as any other kind of worship. There is nothing to say that 'incarnational' worship will not occasionally be escapist or that 'ecstatic' worship can never lead towards an increasing concern for mission and social justice. In fact, this may very often be the case.

There are indeed differences of approach, emphasis and style between these two forms of worship, but I believe that they are not mutually exclusive. In recent years I have tried to cross the barriers between charismatic and alternative worship. At one event, Jonny Baker and I tried to combine worship that was primarily expressed in songs with a series of ritual actions. We used charismatic worship songs in the familiar free-flowing form, but at the same time we offered people the chance to take part in actions, such as drinking water and/or washing their hands in a bowl. What was interesting about these times of worship was that people often found it hard to move from one form of worship to the other. The familiar song-based worship seemed to root them to the spot. It took some encouragement to remind everyone that they were 'free' to go and visit the stations and take part in drinking or washing.

Talking together after the worship times, many people expressed how hard they had found it to move from their seats, but once they had made the effort and found the courage to take part, they found the actions helpful. It would seem that the ecstatic and the incarnational may not be as oppositional as Roberts may be suggesting. At the same time, it is clear that they are both ritualistic 'games', and it can be hard to mix up the rules and create a different form of worship. Creating personalized worship is a very good idea, but people need to have time to learn the rules so that they are able to participate with confidence in the rituals we have designed.

THE EXPRESSIVE AND THE INSTRUMENTAL

A few years back, I was involved in a worship time on the closing day of a conference. Once again, my partner in crime was Jonny Baker. We had set up a variety of worship stations around the church and people were using them to pray and worship. As this was going on, Jonny was playing some dance music through the PA. After a while, I got up with my guitar and started to lead some songs. I could see that for some of those involved, the focus of a few words on an OHP screen and the chance to join in with some songs provided a familiar reference point, and I gathered an enthusiastic crowd (of about 15 people). I sensed that it might be a good idea to ask people to get together and stand in a circle and pray for each other. When I mentioned this to Jonny, he looked at me in horror. 'You can't do that,' he said. 'Why not?' 'You just can't,' he replied. Clearly I had just suggested the most uncool idea! In the end, we didn't do the circle thing and we brought the service to a more postmodern close.

The incident is interesting because it raises a number of issues around the purpose of worship. This, I would suggest, can be seen in terms of a choice: is worship primarily expressive or is it instrumental? What I mean is, do we expect worship to make something happen to those who take part, or does worship simply arise out of the beliefs, actions and sentiments of the group? This question is extremely important because it takes us to an important crossroads in understanding Christian worship. If we see our rituals as being mainly instrumental, then we will expect them to change us in some way. We will join in worship with the expectation that it will bring us into an encounter with God. If ritual is expressive, however, our expectation will not be that worship will change us in some way. Rather, it will sum up the moment or 'express' our communal (or national) feeling. At its best, this approach to worship will also lead to the experience of God—Christ in one another.

My reflex within the worship time at the conference was to seek to create a ritual that would, in some way, express where we were with each other at that time. I wanted not so much to *create* group feeling as to *express* group feeling. My sense was that the decentred worship time didn't create a ritual of leaving. We were left somewhat fragmented at a time when we needed to be joined together. I need to say, by way of a disclaimer, that I am in no way critical of decentred worship times— I love them. Neither am I particularly against a kind of postmodern individualized spirituality—I love it! My point was that, at this moment, what we were offering as worship was doing the wrong thing. I wanted to do something that expressed the mood of the conference.

Jonny's rejection of the idea, I am sure, was based on the fact that it was a bad idea in terms of style. If I had come up with an interesting and original way of expressing ritualistically our oneness at that moment, I am sure he would have been happy to go ahead with it. His reluctance, however, I think, also relates to our growing realization that expressive rituals have been, more often than not, misused. In the hands of the over-enthusiastic worship leader (or, even more sinister, the religious persuader), ritual in worship has been used as a means to create moments of unity and encounter. Religion is easily experienced as manipulation, oppression and abuse in such circumstances. Ritual is never neutral or empty: a simple idea like standing in a circle may seem harmless, but it is rarely that straightforward or, indeed, simple.

Worship is a disputed cultural space. The new forms of personalized ritual that have been developed in recent times have only served to bring into focus and exaggerate the nature of these disputes. From women's groups to gay Christians, from charismatics to those who advocate the use of The Book of Common Prayer, what is clear is that worship is something of a war zone. At the heart of these spiritual culture wars, two main issues are at stake. First, to what extent can each of these styles of worship move us into an awareness of the presence of God? And second, linked to this is the question of common culture and expression in worship: to what extent can a style of worship truly express the beliefs and values of a group?

In the context of worship, the significance of particular actions, words and movements is given a peculiar intensity. In the ritualized world of public worship, our sensitivities are never far below the surface. Worship matters to us, and so we care deeply about these issues. If the worship does not express my own beliefs and yet I feel that I have to join in, I will feel aggrieved. If I sense that, through the worship, someone is trying to manipulate my ideas, and I object to what is being done, then perhaps I will feel that I have been abused. At the same time, worship leaders are always trying to deliver worship that draws people together and expresses a group feeling. There is no escape, therefore, from these particular conflicts.

The challenge for those designing 'personalized ritual' is very clear. On the one hand, worship that is not expressive is dead. On the other, worship that does not seek to be instrumental in some way is frankly something other than worship. At its best, worship will be both instrumental and expressive, but along the way there will be moments of conflict. Teasing out why worship is a war zone may not eliminate all our problems, but it may help to shed light on why a change in style of music, liturgy, seating pattern, or whatever else, has caused us all to get hot under the collar.

THE SOCIALLY CONSTRUCTED AND THE INSPIRED

Over the last two years or so, I have started to lead worship, both in church and also at various conferences. Maybe I should qualify that statement. What I mean is that I have recently started to lead worship in a particular style—charismatic worship. I have always been a bit of a musician, and from time to time I have written songs and used a guitar to lead people in singing these songs as part of worship. What has changed is that now I have consciously tried to adopt a style of worship leading that is recognizably 'charismatic'. The most important thing I have learned from this decision to adopt a particular style is that charismatic worship is a cultural system. What I mean by this is that it is made by people. The 'language' of worship emerges from the collective behaviour of the worshippers and of the worship leader.

I started my transition into what friends have called 'Pete Redman' by observing the way that musicians, particularly those at Soul Survivor, use their music to lead people in worship. From what I could tell, there were a number of musical conventions that seemed to act as signals or triggers to those in the congregation. The most important of these triggers is the way that songs are routinely played to a pattern of crescendo and diminuendo—so most worship songs have loud bits and quiet bits. This means that the worship leader will try to work it so that they build to a loud part, and then follow this by a similar journey towards a quiet bit. This musical dynamic corresponds to a similar journey in the congregation and in the individual worshipper. Loud moments in the worship link to exuberant praise; quiet moments connect to a sense of intimacy and encounter. The repetition of these loud and quiet moments in the worship, I realized from my own experience as a worshipper, allowed me to 'catch a wave' in the worship. If I missed the moment, I knew that it would come around again and I could catch it when it did. Alternatively, if I felt that something significant was happening for me, then I could let the songs and their dynamic wash over me and I could stay with what was of most significance to me.

Observing the way that musical dynamics and spiritual energy interacted, I started to try to replicate this pattern in the way that I was leading. The particular song being sung was generally of less importance than the way that it was played (with 'waves', of course). I realized, as I was learning this, that it was really no different from the alternative worship I had been more used to, or indeed the liturgical worship of my Anglican tradition. In their different ways, all of these forms of worship are made by people and they are, for that reason, cultural. The informal and apparently spontaneous nature of charismatic worship may lend itself to the view that it is a quite different form of worship, but this is not the case. In the informal setting, musical and social conventions are even more important. Without conventions and signals, no one would know where they were. The worship leader, therefore, acts as a kind of conductor, giving clues to where the group might go. This is not the whole picture, however, as I very soon found out.

The worship leader as conductor does not *control* what happens. Many are the times when I have been busy making the waves, trying to indicate where a group should go in the worship, but the group doesn't get the message. In the quiet bits, they just take off and do their own thing, and keep on praising with all their might! Worship leaders at their best have to be responsive, not only giving out signals but also receiving them. This is the way that this culture of worship works. For the casual observer, the importance of the 'charismatic' leader, and the focus on songs led by a band on stage at the front of every meeting, may lead to the conclusion that this is a highly manipulated form of worship, but that fear of 'control' and 'influence', I feel, is often mistaken. I have been at worship events where a huge crowd has gathered, with all of the high-tech video links and PA systems associated with a modern pop concert, but the worship is flat. The band might be very professional and play really well, but worship does not happen. I have concluded from this that communication between worship leaders and congregation lies at the heart of charismatic worship.

In setting out to learn to lead worship, I have never wanted to debunk the mystery of charismatic worship. I understood how the worship worked at a cultural level and I was able to reproduce the signals through my musical appreciation and ability, but this, I knew, did not make me a worship leader. Real worship is worship that is visited by God. Charismatic worship has, as its core value, a concern to encounter God. The worship music and singing are merely the means: they create the ritual space where this meeting can take place. The waves of worship offer a resting place. Like a surfer waiting for the wave, we rest in those moments and wait for the Spirit to lift us into the presence of God. Charismatic worship is therefore a highly personalized kind of ritual, but it must be understood as being not only inspired but also cultural. Social construction can describe the waves and the act of resting, but the work of the Spirit—well, that's another thing.

RITUAL CONNECTIONS

Ritual has power because it takes us beyond ourselves; it connects us to the transcendent. It is for this reason that a totally personalized ritual is less than successful, because in ritual we are searching for God. In a Christian context, even a personalized ritual needs to be located within a theological framework. This does not mean that we are limited to the more regular (and perhaps routinized) rituals of traditional church. What it means is that we need to be conscious of the theological and symbolic interactions that take place as we develop personalized rituals.

A while back, I put together a ritual for use in prayer and public worship. The various elements that made up the ritual were quite simple. I used a shaving mirror, a Bible passage, an icon of the face of Christ and a piece of music. The ritual was designed to be used in a church with a small group (around 20 maximum). On this occasion, there were around 15 people and I encouraged them to gather together around the altar in the sanctuary. I was using an Anglican church that had a fairly formal architecture.

Before the group arrived, I had placed the icon of Christ and the mirror next to each other on the altar. The idea was that when you stood in front of the altar you could see both the icon and your own face reflected in the mirror. The two images would appear side by side and could be viewed at the same time. In front of the icon and the mirror, I placed the Bible, and

I surrounded the Bible, the icon and the mirror with a circle of small candles or nightlights. The Bible was open at 2 Corinthians 3:18, which reads, 'And all of us, with unveiled faces, seeing the glory of the Lord as though reflected in a mirror, are being transformed into the same image from one degree of glory to another; for this comes from the Lord, the Spirit.'

The ritual involved people going up to the altar one at a time. They were asked to read the verse from the Bible and then look at the icon and then in the mirror. While individuals went up to do this, the rest of the group was asked to pray for them. We had no set order for people to go to the altar and there were no other instructions or words. The music used during the ritual came from the soundtrack of *O Brother, Where Art Thou?*, the Coen brothers movie. I took the song by Alison Kraus called 'Down to the River to Pray'. In the movie it is played during a baptism scene and it talks about different groups of people—mothers, fathers, sisters, brothers and sinners—all being invited to go down to the river to pray. It is a short song but I used the repeat button on the CD player so that it would last while we all had a chance to go to the altar. Starting the music marked the beginning of the ritual, and when eventually I faded the music down, this signalled that we had come to its end.

I have used this ritual on a number of occasions, often as part of a conference or when I have been teaching a course on worship. The first time I used it with a group, I was a little taken aback not only by the reaction of those taking part, but also by the power of my own experience. I had dreamed the whole thing up. I knew what was going on. As I prepared everything for the worship time, I had played the music and read the verse and I had looked in the mirror and stared into the face of Christ in the icon. All of this told me that it would 'work'. What it didn't prepare me for was a personal encounter so powerful that it was almost scary. It was a real and transforming encounter with Christ, the one who is changing me into his image from one degree of glory to another. The spiritual energy of the ritual lies, of course, in the work of God and, like anything to do with the Holy Spirit, it is hard to explain. I might have put the right elements together but without the Spirit it was nothing. Still, it is possible to give some indication as to what the right elements may be. In the final section of this chapter I want to reflect upon my experience in designing this personalized ritual and set out what I think were the right elements, which made it so powerful on this occasion.

Rite theology

At the heart of this ritual was the passage from 2 Corinthians. The passage offers a striking theological vision for personal reflection and contemplation. Most importantly, this theological material is from the central root stock of Christian tradition. It is about Christ, who is the image of the Father, and about the Holy Spirit, who is free to change us into that likeness. Here we are told that the glory of God is seen in this work of Christ and in the action of the Spirit. So, in this one verse from Paul's letter, we are taken into the deep truth of the doctrine of the Trinity, and we are also reminded of the work of salvation in the believer. This is heady stuff, but more importantly it is a rich and potent seam where, through prayer and worship, the imagination can be fired and made open to God.

In designing personalized rituals, we will inevitably be looking for something that is new and original. I have nothing against this, but the danger is that in looking for something innovative we search along the margins of the faith, or even for symbols from outside the Christian tradition altogether. While this may not be a bad thing, my own preference is for approaches to ritual that are not just personalized but also an attempt to get deeper into the heart of the Christian faith. The power of this ritual, I believe, was related to its trinitarian nature. Here we were led to contemplate God who is not only mystery but also our salvation.

At the same time, this mysterious element in the ritual was never explained or discussed—it was simply there. I didn't create a clever or complex worship event. It grew from the scripture. 2 Corinthians 3:18 is a complex and ambiguous passage, but my approach was to avoid simplification or explanation. Rather, through the various symbolic elements in the ritual, the ambiguity was explored and to some extent accentuated. The aim was to make space for the theological imagination to flow. Rather than closing down possible interpretations by over-definition, the purpose was to open up the worshipper to the complexity of Christ and his work in our lives. This exposure to the 'word' of God became, in my case and in that of many others, the occasion for God's Spirit to work. I am convinced that this happened because the ritual focused on the richness of the gospel.

Personal and costly

Looking into a mirror sounds simple, but for a great many of us it can be a risky business. We might see our reflection on a daily basis, when we shave or when we do our hair, but this does not mean that we really see ourselves. When we take the time truly to look, it can often be a stranger who looks back at us. The mirror is one way in which we can be confronted by who we are or, perhaps, who we are not. We may not be foolish enough to ask, 'Who is the fairest of them all?' but we are face to face with our own humanity and identity. For these reasons, the mirror in this personalized ritual plays a vital role. It jolts us into 'reality'. We are confronted with ourselves as flesh and bones. We stare into the face of our own mortality.

At the same time, the comparison between the reflection of our selves in the mirror and the face of Christ in the icon raises important questions. Can what I see before me really be in the process of transformation into Christ? As we dwell, even momentarily, on this kind of question, we allow a space for the Spirit to be at work. In such moments, flesh is redeemed. Seeing God at work in our own face is extraordinary. It may take an act of faith and yet it may also strike us 'in the face'. In this ritual, we are not just looking at ourselves. The ritual allows us to look at others as they look. One of those who took part in the worship time commented to me after the service that what moved her most was seeing the faces of people as they stood in front of the mirror. The passage speaks of the reflected glory of Christ on the faces of the believers, and what she saw was the light from the candles flickering on their faces. This reflected light spoke to her of the glory of God at work in the lives of the people who came to pray.

To stand in front of the mirror and then to gaze on the face of Christ was powerful, not just for those taking part but for each of us as we were praying. The energy in the ritual came, in part, from the costly nature of what were doing. We were laying ourselves open and vulnerable to God. This was not easy; it had an emotional cost attached to it. I am more and more convinced that however personalized our rituals may become, they must in some way include this costly element if they are to communicate. I say this because on many occasions I have found the rituals in contemporary worship to be more of a gimmick or a neat idea than a spiritual challenge. Many times, I have not really been challenged by personalized rituals in worship: what we did with the sticky bit of paper and the washing line, or the pebbles and the children's sand tray, or whatever it was that they came up with that week, failed to move me. More often than not, I think this is because the ritual action has no resonance for me at a deeper emotional (and, I suspect, spiritual) level. If we are going to personalize ritual, I do not think that we should do it at the expense of challenge. Ritual can't really be done on the cheap.

Making space for God

A ritual is powerful, I believe, because it makes space where God can move with us and in us. The anthropologist Catherine Bell speaks of the worshipper as a practitioner who moves in ritual space and learns to express themselves within this space.[19] If we want to create personalized rituals that connect with people's desire to worship in new and powerful ways, then we need to pay attention to this idea of movement within a ritualized environment—we need to pay attention to space. In particular, we need to create rituals that take place within a symbolically charged and energized space. The ritual with the mirror and the icon illustrates this idea of 'energized' ritual space in a number of ways.

Firstly, the ritual took place in a traditional church setting. The building and architecture of the church have their own connotations, which were emphasized by the worship taking place around the altar. Moving the whole group from the pews to a less familiar arrangement in the sanctuary was deliberate on my part. The space around the altar, in most Anglican churches, is reserved for the priest, or at least for those designated as being special by wearing some kind of robes. By placing the chairs around the altar, I was pushing at these meanings. There was now no significant divide between the people and the clergy. The congregation, if you like, had taken over the place set aside for the priest. This, I think, sent messages concerning what would happen in the worship time. Here we were sitting in a different place, and something new was going to happen. At the same time, we were close to the 'holy' bit in the church, so maybe it helped to raise the expectation that this would be more spiritually significant than a regular service.

The worshippers were arranged in a circle around the altar. The circle itself is a way of marking space and relationship. Circles are powerful things: they help us to mark inside and outside. Circles in worship join us to each other. This is in contrast to the usual rows facing one or two people at the front of the church. The circle places us all on the same level. It allowed me to lead the worship time but also to participate on an equal footing with the others in the circle.

The circle of worshippers around the altar did not just symbolize joining together in worship. It also worked powerfully in another way. The worship time started with a completed circle and ended with a completed circle. As the ritual progressed, individuals moved from being part of the circle to the centre of attention. In terms of practice, the worshipper starts as part of a group and 'goes solo' journeying to the altar. At the centre of the circle, they become the centre of our attention. My own experience was that this journey was very significant. I was intensely aware that people were looking at me and praying for me as I came to read the Bible at the altar.

At the centre of the circle of worshippers we came to another sacred space. The use of the nightlights on the altar served as a further signal that this was something special. Around the Bible, the icon and mirror, I had created another 'inner circle'—a ring of light. Light symbolizes the glory of God that rests in the holy place. Coming towards the altar was therefore a journey towards glory, the presence of God.

Ritual space was designated not just by the seating arrangements or the candles or the church building. Sacred space was also created in this worship by the way that we set aside a moment in time. We entered into the ritual and exited the ritual as a group. My role was to explain how things were meant to work. I always liken this to the setting up of a game of Monopoly or chess. The cards or playing pieces go on the board, everyone gets the bits they need, the money is laid out in the bank and eventually all the pieces are lined up. This takes time but it is not really part of the action. It is only when the first white pawn is moved or when the dice is thrown that the game begins. Beginning the game signals a new kind of order coming into operation.

For sacred ritual, this new order is a journey into a place of divine transformation. Entering such a space is often intimidating, so I try to look for ways to invite participation. The song 'Down to the River to Pray' was used because the performance is enticing and seductive. It calls us to get out of our seat and plunge into the river, because it is in the river that we can pray. The invitation in song started when I turned the CD on and it ended when I faded the music out. Ritual was marked in both space and also in time. Music is one of the key ways in which we can mark out time for ritual encounter.

4. Corporate and individual

What we know as alternative worship (or alt.worship) in this country has mostly evolved from a reaction against evangelicalism and the charismatic movement. In particular, people have found corporate forms of worship, especially chorus singing, to be a really big turn-off. In its place, groups have sought to emphasize more individualized or decentred forms of spirituality and prayer. The Labyrinth is a good example of this. I am very enthusiastic about this kind of prayer and worship. The problem with some kinds of personalized ritual, in my view, is that they are in danger of selling individualism. I am concerned that we should not lose the corporate elements in worship. But I am also very enthusiastic about designed and personalized rituals. This is something of a problem, and getting a balance in one worship time is very often impossible.

I suppose I want to challenge charismatic and alt.worship and push the boundaries of both. Where charismatic worship might have an over-emphasis upon worship that is led from the front and based on a high level of corporate activity, especially singing, I want to see some more space for individual spiritual journeys and rituals. With the alt.worship groups, I feel there should be space for corporate activity (especially singing).

The mirror and icon ritual was designed to allow for the expression of both corporate and individual forms of worship to be exercised at the same time. The circle of prayer around the altar emphasized the body of believers and the power of prayer with other people. The journey into the centre of that prayer, however, was individual. Here the encounter with the face of Christ was one on one. The energy in the ritual, I think, came from the individual aspect of getting up, reading the Bible passage and looking in the mirror and at the icon, but this energy was magnified by the corporate prayer.

The increase in ritualized forms of worship is highly significant, not least because it is evident in so many different groups of Christians (and, indeed, non-Christians). It is extremely important, therefore, that we start to reflect upon what is happening as we worship in these new and varied ways. We must not let personalized ritual go unexamined.

There needs to be more discussion of this topic. For instance, I have not touched on weddings or funerals. These are clearly two of the few places where 'non-believers' or those who are outside of regular churchgoing attempt to personalize ritual. There must be an attempt made to gather examples of these forms of religious expression and reflect upon them theologically. Analysis, I believe, should lead us to a renewed practice in our own worship and in the way that worship connects to mission. This chapter has argued for a nuanced and continuing theological reflection upon the way that worship is developing through personalized ritual in the church. This kind of reflection is not just an academic exercise; it is actually essential to the creative process.

BLACK STYLES, RITUALS AND MISSION FOR THE 21ST CENTURY

Anthony Reddie

WHERE WE AT?

In this chapter I want to take an innovative look at the phenomena of Black youth and issues surrounding identity and belonging. I want to suggest that an understanding of the rituals associated with Black styles and cultural appropriations offers us an important matrix for the development of appropriate 'rites of passage' models for youth mission in the 21st century.

In this first section I want to map out the contours of Black identity and culture, showing the extent to which Black expression and ontology is a rich, vibrant and complex matrix of rituals and codified practice. Before we can get into this segment of the argument, we need to look at some of the background stuff—in effect, 'Where we at?'

The role of young people in British society, particularly Black youth, has always been a problematic one. Any approach that seeks to engage with Black youth needs to be informed by the historical factors that led to the systematic negation of the Black self. The work of Robert Beckford, for example, has highlighted the historic breach between White hegemony and the objectification and demonization of the Black self.[20]

In its dealings with Black youth, the British state has often pathologized such individuals. This pathologizing often leads to particular roles being imposed upon Black youth—roles that are predicated on the often un-spoken assumption that deviancy and maladjusted behaviour are the natural accompaniments of Black youth and their perceived status in British society. Black people have long been seen as a problem for the British state.[21] Writers such as Tony Sewell, for example, have analysed Black young men in the British school system and the many forces that impinge upon this section of society.[22]

The disparity between Black cultural display and reality and the claims of White power and influence has always been problematic. Black people remain past masters of subversion, secrecy and signifying. In effect, attempts to pigeonhole and constrict us have met with a form of defiance that is manifested in numerous ways.[23]

Attempting to gauge the cultural aesthetics and selfhood of Black youth requires a sophisticated and engaged form of negotiation between those wanting to gain access and the subject who may want to conceal or withdraw. The relative failure of the institutional churches' mission when juxtaposed with contemporary Black experience has been their inability to penetrate the subversive world of Black codes, manners and behaviour and their accompanying patterns that are an inherent feature of Black existence. This insurmountable barrier becomes all the more pernicious when it is placed within the context of relations between church and Black youth.[24] In volume two of my book, *Growing into Hope*, I outline the common experience of Black alienation from the ongoing mission of the Church, particularly in terms of White ecclesiology. In an early section of the book, I speak of a phenomenon I have termed 'Dancing at home and dancing abroad'. This exercise was created in order to describe the disparities between White 'correctitute' and Black 'subversive alienation'.[25]

The failure of missiological approaches in the postmodern epoch has been their inability to engage with the emotional struggles of the Black experience. The almost total focus upon doctrine and dogmatics, at the expense of relevant pastoral care and liberative action (praxis), has led to a diminution of the emotional concerns of postmodern youth (the affective) in favour of the need to have specific truth claims and knowledge (the cognitive).[26] Attempts to instil right belief and Christian teaching have negated the importance of relating to the emotional and psycho-social realities of being a marginalized, excluded 'other'.

While not wishing to discount the importance of developing patterns of thinking and knowledge (cognitive frames of reference) for the teaching and learning process, my concern lies principally in the area of the affective—namely, the emotional development of young people. James Michael Lee reminds us that it has been fashionable for social scientists to subordinate the affective in favour of the cognitive, as the latter is seen as a resource that can be trusted. The affective (the emotional and feelings parts of being human), by contrast, is understood to be ephemeral, vague and based too much on emotion. The affective is not to be trusted and is in many ways the antithesis of the cognitive processes that play a crucial role in the development of our human awareness. Lee, however, proceeds by stating that 'the path to humanity and to divinity lies not through power or politics or cognition, but through affect and value and love. Thus it behoves the religious educator to centre a good deal of his attention on the affective content of religious instruction.'[27]

Reflecting upon my own experiences as a first point of departure, I am aware of the ways in which this issue was an ongoing feature of my own formative experiences, back in the early 1980s. My own sense of alienation and disaffection from the overarching symbols of Whiteness in the Christian faith is replicated in a younger generation of Black youth. The teaching and underlying theology of the Christian faith as expressed by White Europeans had dug deep into the wounded psyche of countless numbers of Black youth in Britain.

Pioneers in developing a contextualized approach to the Christian education and mission of Black youth were James M. Jones and M. Lee Montgomery. These authors, as far back as 1970, advocated that effective Christian education and mission among such marginalized and disaffected groups must be holistic and have as a central concern the emotional well-being of the Black child. This emotional well-being is bound up with the search for a positive identity.[28]

Mission for the 21st century has to incorporate a thematic and pedagogical template that is attuned to the cultures, identities, historical and contemporary experiences and expressions of Black people. This approach to the Christian faith will be alive to the socio-political and economic realities of inner-city life in Britain.

A Black, African-centred approach to mission and pastoral care has to cope with the fault-lines that separate and distort the humanity of Black youth. This dichotomy has given rise to an ongoing feature of Black life, particularly within White majority-dominated societies. That feature is the seemingly all-pervasive issue of cultural dissonance. The cultural dissonance exhibited in Black life is a component of the ongoing reality that is, in part, an indicator of Black selfhood and identity. The indications of Black selfhood and identity are often represented by 'what you are not' rather than who you are in a positive sense. Namely, as a Black person, I am defined by the fact that I am not White: in a White-dominated society and world, I am perceived as the 'other'. This experience of marginalization and exclusion is one that is beyond the imaginings of most White people.

James Baldwin extends this point very well when writing about his own formative experiences.[29] Baldwin criticizes the failures of White social scientists to understand the world of the Black person and to appreciate how one's perception of that world defines one's social reality. All too often, White social scientists have attempted to interpret Black life through the filter of White power and influence.[30]

Similarly, in his work researching Black young people, Mairtin Mac an Ghaill has highlighted concerns that are not dissimilar to those perceived by Baldwin. Mac an Ghaill writes, 'White social science research has made problematic dominated social groups such as the Black community. Furthermore, the researchers have used their cultural power to define the dominated groups' social worlds.'[31]

The methodological approach I am advocating not only has to be informed by the split, separated nature of Black life, but also needs to find a way of penetrating the social realities of Black life in an authentic and engaged fashion. I believe that a form of mission for this new century must be personally engaged, trying to move beneath the skin of the Black self to the psyche of the separated African soul in which there is a struggle between 'two unreconciled strivings; two warring ideals in one dark body, whose dogged strength alone keeps it from being torn asunder'.[32]

Discovering where we at

In all forms of youth ministry, practitioners and researchers are expected to get their hands dirty. This means that in order to work alongside Black youth, they need to be engaged—to be immersed in the social context and the whole-view of the young people with whom they are attempting to work. An assumed maxim of ethnographic work, for example, particularly in the use of participant observation, is the notion of social interaction with the context and significant others within that specific environment.

To what extent, however, can White youth ministry specialists climb beneath the skin of Black youth? I would argue that this is extremely doubtful, if not impossible. In my current publication, *Faith, Stories and the Experience of Black Elders: Singing the Lord's Song in a Strange Land*, I have sought to investigate the oral traditions of Black people. These oral traditions are the means by which people of the African diaspora have learnt what it is to be Black human beings through the medium of Black storytelling and experience.[33] I have asserted that these stories of faith and experience developed as a means of countering the worst excesses of White control and power that played an integral role in the dehumanization of Black self-identity.[34]

One of the means of discovering 'where we at' is by means of structured conversations with Black youth, attempting to discern what are the situational dilemmas and major themes that are operative in their lives. While there are many who have remained deeply sceptical about the claims of James Fowler's schema for faith development[35] (indeed, I would count myself as one of them), nevertheless this concept has proved helpful in enabling practical theologians to gain a sense of how faith works in the context of human life.

Fowler's schema is concerned more with the 'how' of faith than the 'what' of faith—that is, how faith is constructed as opposed to what is the content of people's faith. I cite the work of James Fowler because, in my previous research, I was anxious to make use of some of his ideas in order to find ways of penetrating aspects of the identity and existence of Black youth.[36] In particular, I wanted to create a method by which youth practitioners, pastors and religious educators might be enabled to discover the latent concerns and issues at play in the life experiences of Black youth. Often, these issues have their antecedents in the ongoing historical struggle of people of African descent to embrace their Blackness in a world where Whiteness is privileged and represents the norm. In creating the 'Oral Tradition Document',[37] I have created a mechanism that enables Black youth to engage in dialogue with their elders, to revisit the past so that they can remake the present and, I hope, change the future.[38]

This existing research has been undertaken in order to discover ways of alerting religious practitioners to the realities of discovering where we at.

The importance of attempting to document and describe the social and cultural environment in which the sense of being, knowledge of the world, and the areas in which authority resides for Black youth should not need elaborate analysis. The age-old maxim, 'You cannot redeem that which you do not know', remains a critical truth for all youth practitioners and researchers. Although, in my own work, I have used social scientific theories in my attempt to climb beneath the skin of Black denial and signifying, it can be argued that this approach to the process of contextualization and critical social analysis[39] is not new. Paul's encounter with the Greeks in Athens in the first century was, in many respects, a classic case of understanding and interpreting the philosophical worldview and ideological concerns of an articulate Gnostic culture.[40] I would argue that this process is one that is central to Pauline theology. Christianity needs to understand before it can reclaim.[41]

KNOWING WHERE WE AT, WHAT HAPPENS NOW?

Having attempted to discover 'where we at', we come to the taxing question of action. What are we to do with such knowledge? For what reason have we delved beneath the surface? Simply to write books and fashion a reputation as a cultural commentator and media darling? Many have trodden this well-walked route to becoming a crowned expert and sage.

In the case of Black youth ministry, I am arguing that the possession of such knowledge is not simply an end in itself, but rather it is a missiological enterprise. A knowledge of the rituals and cultic patterns of association inherent within Black popular culture can enable the enterprising informal educator to fashion appropriate pedagogical approaches to the mission of the church and her engagement with Black youth. In the next section of this chapter, I want to highlight a fictional dramatization based upon a real-life interaction between a group of Black youths. This sketch was written in order to provide a reflective mirror on aspects of Black popular culture for Black youth. Following the dramatic presentation of this material, a period of reflection and analysis ensued between the young people and the youth leader.

Set inside a small living-room. Two Black women are deep in conversation. It is nearing midnight.

Woman 1:	*(African origin)* So tell me sis, whah appenin Saturday?
Woman 2:	*(African origin also)* Me no know… Yu have anyting plan?
Woman 1:	Not ah ting… Me do wi some excitement. Yu know of any dance ah tek place?
Woman 2:	No.

The door opens and in walks a young White woman, carrying a tray full of hot drinks. She places them on the floor and joins the other two.

Woman 3:	There you go. Two teas and a coffee. Help yourself to biscuits.
Woman 1:	*(To Woman 3)* What have you got planned for Saturday? Only Carol and me couldn't think of anything to do.
Woman 3:	Well, apart from going to the hairdressers, nothing.
Woman 1:	So you'll be busy all day then?
Woman 3:	*(Slightly taken aback)* No… won't take much longer than half an hour or so.
Woman 1&2:	*(In unison)* What?
Woman 3:	Yeah… It's only a haircut.
Woman 2:	Only a haircut? You hear dis Susan? Only a haircut.
Woman 1:	Joke she ah joke. Jus a haircut.
Woman 3:	*(Playing with long strands of her hair)* I don't do much with it… I have the fringe cut down and the split ends removed. Only a quick job.
Woman 1:	Well that's news to me. Do you mean that's it? You simply go in, have your end snipped away and then walk out?
Woman 3:	*(Almost apologetically)* Yes.
Woman 2:	Yu is a lucky 'oman… I wish I could simply snip a little of me head to look good. Yu would be shocked if you knew how me much me spen on mi head.
Woman 1:	That no nothin'. Las week, me spen ah whole day on mi backside inah de hairdressers. My bottam was so sore, me

	couldn't walk fi three weeks afterwards. And when de 'oman finish, mi head still look hugly.
Woman 2:	De las time mi did go to the hairdressers, dis feisti 'oman put a whole heap of chemical inah me head. Tink? Bwoy, yu should ah smell mi when dem finish? Dem nasty up me head so much, me did have to tek ah plastic bag and cover mi self. Me shame 'til me nearly dead.
Woman 3:	This may seem a silly question. But why do you go to such lengths for a simple haircut?
Woman 2:	Nothing simple about it. We have fi change our style often. As me Mumma always says, 'If you wan good, den yu nose mus run.'
Woman 3:	(Slightly confused) Yes…
Woman 1:	And after all, if yu want fi ketch ah man, yu mus look good. Good men hard fi find.
Woman 3:	I've never had that problem. I like my hair long and see no need to change it. And as for men, they either like my hair as it is or else they can take a walk.
Woman 1:	Yes, but you're talking about white men. They're not as fussy as black guys.
Woman 2:	Nobody has an ego as big as a black man's. I once knew this black guy who was only five foot six, but his ego was still six feet tall. He had to measure himself a new pair of trousers to fit it in.
Woman 1:	Don't talk to me about black men. Dem all fufool duppy idiots wi no sense, bad attitudes and no respect fi women.

There is a knock at the door. Woman 3 gets up to answer it. Enter a Black man. He joins the three women in the room.

Man:	(Jovially) Hi y'all.
Woman 1:	(To Woman 2) See 'im day.
Man:	(Nervously) Hmmmm… Have I done something wrong? Just that I detect a little hostility in here.
Woman 3:	(To man) Look at Carol and Susan… As a man, what do you think about their hair?
Man:	Is this a trick question?
Woman 3:	How would you say it compared to mine?

Man:	I don't know it's different. They'd look stupid with your hair. I don't think Rapunzel was a black woman.
Woman 3:	(*Probing*) If you were going out with one of them...
Woman 2:	Being a black man, he'd be going out with both of us.
Woman 1:	At the same time.
Man:	(*Trying to protest his innocence*) Hey, now wait on a minute...
Woman 3:	Just let's assume you were going out with one of them. Would you expect them to change their hair often?
Man:	Hmm... It would depend... Hard to say.
Woman 3:	But if you were going out with me... a white woman. Would you expect me to change my hair at all?
Man:	Call me cynical if you want, but I suspect a plot here. I'm keeping stumb. I've known men get verbal lashings for saying the wrong thing at a time like this. I'm standing on the third amendment.
Woman 2:	And what's that?
Man:	I have the right to remain silent, if in testifying I'm likely to incriminate myself.
Woman 2:	Coward.
Man:	What's this about anyway? I only came around for some takeaway. You lot invited me as well. If I had known you were going to put me through the Spanish Inquisition, I'd have stayed back at my yard.
Woman 1:	So you're not fussy about the women you date and their hairstyles?
Man:	I date so few women, I can afford to be fussy.
Woman 2:	Nice try, but the playing-for-sympathy angle won't wash.
Man:	Look, I'm not fussy what a woman does with her hair. I'm not a hair man.
Woman 1:	So if I was to shave my head bald like a julee mango, you'd still buy me a drink at a dance?
Man:	Sure I'd still buy you a drink... of toilet water.
Woman 2:	Yu too lie. You jus said yu nah partial 'bout hairstyle.
Woman 3:	That's what you said... I heard you loud and clear.
Man:	What is this? Give-men-a-hard-time week?
Woman 3:	We sisters have got to stick together.
Woman 2:	So you wouldn't date a bald woman?
Man:	Come on, let's start living in the real world. You've got to

	draw the line somewhere. I have nothing against bald women. In fact...
Woman 3:	Don't tell me, some of your best friends are bald women.
Man:	Let me explain...
Woman 1:	What about women with locks?
Woman 2:	Women with shaven down sides?
Woman 3:	Women with bright lime green streaks down the middle?
Woman 1:	Women with maps of Africa tattooed to their cranium?
Woman 2:	Women with silly messages etched on to their forehead?
Woman 3:	Like 'Mam and Dad' and 'love and hate'?
Woman 1:	And 'Kev loves Sharon'.
Woman 2:	And 'Derek woz 'ere'.
Woman 3:	What about... What about... a woman, with no hair, no head, three noses, a side parting and a gold medallion, saying, 'Freedom is coming, oh yes I know'?
Man:	This is ridiculous.
Woman 2:	Answer the question.
Woman 1:	Or are you like all the men we know? Prejudiced beyond belief.
Man:	(Rising to his feet and getting ready to go) Well if you bring these women along, I'll date them all.
Woman 2:	You going somewhere?
Man:	Back to my yard, where I won't get no boderation.

The man gets to his feet and storms out of the room... we hear the front door slam. There follows a few seconds of silence.

Woman 3:	Touchy touchy.
Woman 2:	What did we say?
Woman 1:	I never said a word.
Woman 2:	Men! Didn't I tell you? So fragile and egotistical. You daren't say a word to them.
Woman 3:	Oh well, can't be helped... At least there's more takeaway for everyone else.
Woman 1:	(To Woman 3) By the way Carole, how are you having your hair done?
Woman 3:	The usual. Have the fringe snipped off and the ends trimmed.

Woman 2:	Twenty-minute job?
Woman 3:	Yep.
Woman 1:	Yu lucky wretch.

We hear someone banging at the window. Woman 3 goes to window and draws back the curtain. We see the man outside peering in through the window.

Man:	*(Shouting through window)* What do you mean by prejudiced beyond belief? Are you saying that I'm a prejudiced person? Not that I'm hyper-sensitive in any way, but what exactly are you saying?
Woman 3:	*(Re-draws the curtains, ignoring the man)* Now where were we?
Woman 2:	Talking about your hair Carole... Tell me, how do you get it to look so flexible and manageable like that?
Woman 3:	Well, I swear by Timotei natural conditioner. I find it so soft and gentle and it doesn't ruin the environment either.
Woman 1:	Oh you don't say.
Woman 2:	Isn't that nice?
Woman 3:	I'll lend you some of mine if you like.
Man:	*(Screaming from outside)* I'm not prejudiced. It's a filthy lie. I'll see you in court fi dis...*

The end.

WE KNOW WHERE WE AT AND HAVE SEEN WHAT CAN BE DONE: SO WHAT NOW?

This final section is an attempt to reflect upon the drama *Crucial Cuts*. The themes within the sketch are drawn from the many styles and rituals of Black life. The use of this dialogue is important, because it provides a method of engagement that moves us away from the polite discussion model of youth ministry that seems the norm in democratic Western societies. In my previous research, I was struck by the extent to which White, eurocentric models of Christian education would presume a certain level of compliance and engagement with the educative process.[42] Black youth, particularly those from marginalized and disaffected backgrounds in inner-city urban contexts, whose experiences in school are largely negative, will not permit themselves to reflect passively while some well-intentioned informal educator seeks to impart 'truths' to them. In fairness, the movements in postmodern Christian youthwork and ministry have begun to shed the tired clichés of the 1960s' incarnational coffee-bar, table-tennis-playing model of informal education.

This scripted playlet was designed to enable Black youth to discuss a variety of concerns and issues that are prevalent in contemporary postcolonial Britain. The sketch enables youth practitioners to utilize their understanding of 'where we at' and the action that might arise from such knowledge. In the first instance, the young people are invited to re-enact the scripted scenario. The more experienced members are encouraged to improvise and add their own lines in light of their experiences. The sketch is performed on at least three or four occasions. Not only are the participants encouraged to enter into the characterizations, but those observing are placed into support groups, in order to identify with particular characters or issues as they arise during the re-enactment of the sketch.

In order to enable Black youth to move beyond the self-conscious limitations of being Black in a White-dominated world, dramatizations such as *Crucial Cuts* are an essential resource. Neutral or generic learning materials created in order to further the churches' historic mission to witness to the life-changing truths of Jesus Christ tend to reinforce the marginalized and demonized status of Black people in Britain.[43] As the great Paulo Freire reminds us, neutral education is impossible.[44] All forms of education are ideological enterprises and the mission and ministry of the church is no different.[45] We simply have to ask which sections of society have benefited from the domestication of the Christian faith for the ideological, top-down, patrician element of the churches' mission to become readily apparent.[46]

How does *Crucial Cuts* work?

Crucial Cuts invites Black youth to become active participants in the process of learning and relearning aspects of their existence and experience. Using an experiential and participatory method of working, Black youth become the central 'actors' in a process of reflecting upon scenarios and contexts that speak to their experiences of being Black in Britain. The sketch works due to the writer's knowledge of the issues at play in the lives of these Black young people.

The preceding sections of this chapter, are in effect, an overarching philosophy and pedagogy for the need to gain subjective insider knowledge of the needs and concerns of Black youth (knowing where we at) in order to construct dramatic learning opportunities such as *Crucial Cuts*. In using this material, we are attempting to find a mechanism that will allow pictures of the reality of Black youth to become readily apparent. The days of 'massa knows best', or the paternalistic ideals of conservatively minded leaders who 'police' their own on behalf of the state,[47] are long gone— thankfully, I might add! Instead, a postmodern generation cannot simply be told, but wants to be convinced or wants to know why.[48] While some decry this state of affairs, I feel it offers a more healthy and realistic context in which the church can engage in its mission. In another piece of writing, I have argued that the church, in the form of its leaders or those who work on its behalf, needs to earn the right to be respected and taken seriously.[49]

In using this sketch, I have sought not to impose or to assume. The only supposition I have permitted myself is the presumption to write this dramatic piece in the first instance. *Crucial Cuts* was written in order that certain truths about some of the concerns and issues of Black urban life could become more visible and so be challenged and critiqued by the transforming power that is the gospel of Christ—in effect, redeeming what we have come to understand or, perhaps more realistically, understanding more clearly than we did before.

Following the repeated re-enactments of the sketch, the young people are encouraged to break into groups to debrief. What are some of the issues that have arisen from the repeated playing of the sketch? Who is affirmed? Why does the man behave the way he does? How much of a unifying concept is gender? Are all women the same? Who normally holds power in incidences such as these?

On a number of occasions, the young people have been encouraged to reflect upon Jesus' interaction with women depicted in the Gospels. Are there any similarities or differences, for example, between Jesus and the woman at the well and the incident depicted in *Crucial Cuts*? This sketch attempts to draw out some of the nascent themes of Black youth culture in a postmodern context. In doing so, it seeks to highlight the Black styles and rituals for mission in the 21st century.

What are the themes in *Crucial Cuts* that can be highlighted?

The use of language in the sketch is interesting in that the Black young people are depicted using Jamaican Creole.[50] Writers such as Tomlin have highlighted the cultural, liturgical and political importance of 'Black language' in the linguistic and emotional repertoire of Black people.[51] Black linguistic styles are essential to the development and identity formation of Black youth.

Janice Hale, in her pioneering work with Black children in the United States, argues that the intellectual processes of knowing (cognition) are not only shaped by biological growth and development (maturation), but are also influenced by culture.[52] The way of life and context in which people are socialized has a direct bearing upon how they see the world and their development as human persons. A recent article by Lerleen Willis, a Black linguistic scholar at Nottingham Trent University, investigates the relationship between Black idioms such as Patois or Jamaican Creole and the Black identity construction and positioning of Black youth in post-millennium Britain.[53]

In additional to the use of language, the sketch touches upon themes such as gender, particularly relations between Black and White women. Writers such as Jil Brown,[54] Lorraine Dixon[55] and Jacquelyn Grant[56] have commented upon the disparities between Black and White women. The central theme of the sketch is the often contentious area of Black hair—its aesthetics, socio-cultural politics and connotations of identity. The divergence between politics of Black women's hair and their erstwhile

White peers is a stark one. Sewell has commented on the wider cultural and political factors that come into play when discussing the type of cuts or styles employed in Black display.[57] Robert Beckford has argued that the stylistic innovations and modifications of Black hair and its representation can serve as an important barometer in the post-colonial developments of Black self-identity.[58] Similarly, in the sexual politics between the Black women and the Black man, we have a microcosm for the ongoing gender discourse within Black popular culture that is an important feature of a great deal of current cultural commentary.[59]

A new approach to Black youth ministry will use these forms of dialogical role-play as a means of highlighting socio-cultural issues that are prevalent within Black culture. By reflecting back to the young people's elements of Black style and ritual, we are able to critique these cultural traits and bring them into conversation with the gospel. We have started from being on the outside looking in, to a point where we have seen 'where we at', to an end point of being able to reflect back and critique. The use of *Crucial Cuts* is to stimulate laughter and engagement with Black style and ritual, from a subjective insider perspective.

Of course, to be able to undertake this form of creative writing (and documentation) and reflective dialogical process, one needs to be an insider. You need to know 'where it's at' and 'what it's all about'. Yet, the efficacy of this approach is one that allows this process to bring the power of the gospel alive through the cultural aesthetics that are a central part of the experience of being a young Black person in 21st-century Britain. Time and space do not permit an ongoing discussion about how the gospel of Christ can be incarnated through Black popular culture, while transforming and critiquing the very medium through which it is operating. That is for another occasion. At this point, I simply say, 'I'm outta here' or, in Black speak, 'Mi garn!'

CURIOSITY... GAVE THE CAT NINE LIVES

Ana Draper

Mention the word 'worship', and you might be tempted to think of an out-of-tune guitarist strumming 'Shine Jesus Shine', or an organist diving feet-first into a rousing rendition of 'All Things Bright and Beautiful'. It's not always like that, of course. Some expressions of worship are beautiful and inspiring, but most Christians, if we're honest, have grown frighteningly used to the culture in which we express our faith—with its rituals that are at best out of date and at worst irrelevant. Isn't it time we stopped to think what in God's name we are doing?

CURIOSITY

The church has often been so keen to defend its answers that, over time, it has forgotten what the questions were in the first place. 'Who are we?' (or, more specifically, 'What is church?') is one. 'What's the point of worship?' is another. In asking such questions, we force ourselves to face old matters head-on within our strange, new cultures; and we also engage a few simple yet profound principles used by psychotherapists. The first, we call 'curiosity'.

Curiosity never allows you to sit pretty, to rest on your laurels. It forbids presumptions and assumptions about the way things are. It drives us onward to understand who we are, why we're here and where we're going. It is a brilliantly simple tool that need not be restricted to therapeutic practice, but can be applied to our lives and to the life and faith of the church.

Curiosity provokes an ongoing search for truth, not an arrogant assumption that we have found it, distilled it and bottled it. It demands openness to new ideas instead of a defence of the old. It opens up dialogue instead of closing debate. For Christians, it helps us view creation through fresh and wondering eyes each day instead of sitting life out in anticipation of future rescue from this wicked world.

Curiosity also demands that we think again about 'worship'. Is it really just a 20-minute musical interlude in an otherwise dreary service? That's what we have grown used to, but curiosity does not permit us to grow used to anything. How might worship look if we dreamed it up again— if we opened up the possibilities, to see every aspect of our lives as a potential act of worship to a God with whom we are in relationship?

Might it look like commuting to work every morning? Sharing a meal, playing football or going to a concert? Sitting by the sea? Staring at the stars? Living, breathing, loving? Such worship requires us not to arrive and settle but to travel, and in the process to transform into sacred space every place where we live, every room in which we work, every relationship we share.

This is to make both the sacred mundane and the mundane sacred; to smash through the secular–sacred divide, the division between the things of God and not of God; to express mystery and transcendence through the ordinary objects of life, like bread and wine; to express our life journeys through stories lived and told; to celebrate our becoming, our growing and our being in relationship with ourselves, God, each other and the earth.

Systemic psychotherapists seek to understand the system or context within which we derive our self-understanding. Our relationships help to put worship in its true place; they should provide its real context and imbue it with meaning. We are defined by our relationships with others: born as individuals, our task is to become persons, and there is no limit to becoming more truly personal. In becoming who we are, we engage in an active and ongoing act of worship, seeing ourselves continually transformed and playing a part in the transformation of others.

A therapist will tell you that it's crucial to remain curious in any relationship—about the person, about their situation, about who they are becoming—to listen instead of talk; to ask questions instead of giving answers. Jesus frequently asked questions of those he encountered. The supposedly all-knowing God seemed ever curious about real people, in a way that transformed their situations.

If the interconnectedness of our lives forms the very stuff of worship, then the rituals we develop—whether everyday habits or grander, more formal collective acts—help to reflect this. They express our corporate stories and evolve within our ongoing relationships. Therapists understand the transformative power of rituals, and will specifically encourage families to create new ones in order to move on. When one woman felt guilty about the death of her son, she started to tell her husband about how big the guilt was and what it looked like. He, in turn, would tell her stories about her mothering, her love for her child, and he would remind her of the professionals who said that there was nothing they could have done to save their son. This was their 'guilt ritual'; and in this way guilt became something they could control, make sense of and share.

Rituals can evolve from metaphors. One client had experienced every type of bereavement—the deaths of a parent, wife, best friend and child. He believed he held a 'doctorate in grief', and pictured life as a card game in which he'd been dealt a terrible hand. Together, we co-created a ritual in which we named the cards he now held in his hand (his son, his successful career, his doctorate in grief, his new wife...), and it was then that he started to imagine new ideas about what life could be like and how he could continue to live positively.

In raising curiosity about the new possibilities that are open to us and to those with whom we share our lives, we can help to transform the pain (or just the inertia of the ordinary), with the help of ritual and metaphor, by creating hope for new futures. This is a truly liberating perspective in which the secular and the sacred need never be separate, but intertwined and indivisible.

NEUTRALITY

Systemic psychotherapists also place great importance on the need for 'neutrality'—that is, remaining as neutral as possible within any given therapeutic situation. They acknowledge their intrinsic lack of objectivity —everyone, of course, has assumptions, preconceptions, value systems and beliefs which affect how we see the world—but they try as hard as possible not to let it predetermine their understanding of any situation.

This is hard, but also liberating, for Christians who have a tendency to view everything through their own lenses. A group of us were invited by a Christian charity to train people working with families who were affected/infected by HIV/AIDS, and when we proposed that one of the key areas we would like to introduce to their work was neutrality, they became anxious. Most of the workers were Christian, and the organ-ization feared that they would be unable to adopt a neutral position with families—it meant for some that they would need to suspend their urge to find immediate resolution through conversion, or prayer for healing, for example, or to judge people strictly in terms of their own Christian worldview.

It is very hard for anyone, let alone Christians, to approach any situation from a neutral position. But in striving to do so, and in raising our curiosity about the people with whom we are relating, we are likely to learn far more about them, and act with a much greater measure of grace, than if we presume that we know the answers to their problems and seek to impose those answers. Of course, if we apply such a principle to our faith, we are likely to view each new situation, each challenge or opportunity, through fresh eyes. How might church better apply to a postmodern society, for example? If we remain neutral about what church might be for, or what it potentially could achieve, then our past anxieties about its ineffectuality or the harm it causes can be put aside. Similarly, if we hold traditional views about worship, and refuse to look afresh at our new context, then we will only consider solutions that are based entirely within our traditional paradigm. We will also be far more likely to be judgmental about our changing world, and more defensive about the role of the church in society, than if we are willing to approach the new culture with neutrality.

A pastor once refused to marry a member of his congregation because she had been divorced. He made a judgment that to be divorced and to remarry was a sinful thing. Yet he had only ever known a faithful wife and a relatively happy marriage. In viewing this woman through his own experience of marriage, he was unable to express compassion or allow her to enter into grace. If he had spoken to her from a position of neutrality, he may have discovered that she had worked hard at her first marriage. He may have heard stories of a young man (the man she now wanted to marry) being willing to become father to another man's children. He may have heard about regret and repentance at the things that went wrong in the past. In hearing these stories, he may have formed a different viewpoint, one based on remaining in relationship with the couple, which in turn creates the possibility of a changed story—perhaps of a man who loves not only a woman but also her children, or a woman who is loved and discovers faithfulness. The woman would then become beloved and not rejected.

CIRCULARITY

From positions of neutrality and curiosity, systemic psychotherapists also seek to ask circular questions, which don't always get directly to the point, and which rarely leave room for a simple yes-or-no answer. Therapists seldom ask, 'Why?' (which is called a 'closed' question) because it leaves little room for an alternative, transformative story to emerge. Circular questions allow both parties very effectively to explore a much broader range of responses to their situation instead of settling swiftly on a premeditated solution or answer. As in the therapeutic situation, so with our general approach to life: if we ask more questions of any person or situation, and if we refuse to draw from others the responses they think we expect or would like to hear, then we will learn far more and will open ourselves and others up to a much wider range of possibilities.

As Christians, we need to learn to ask questions that take into account more of our differences. (To begin to ask questions of each other at all would probably be a start.) It might be that you are a man and I am a woman; I am an artist and you are a mathematician; I lived with indigenous Indians in Ecuador, and you have always lived in London. My parents may have adopted street children, and you have a natural brother; I never met my grandparents, you are very close to yours; and so on. These differences create the values, ideas and rules that govern our lives; to say that we are the same would be to pretend there is no difference between us. It is because of our differences that we need to ask questions that bring meaning and context to our actions and interactions.

Obviously, psychotherapists are trained to ask questions, but anyone can help others to imagine new possibilities and futures, simply by avoiding the temptation to ask leading questions that will bring them round to your way of thinking. Wouldn't it be liberating if, instead of being told what to do by your minister or leader on a Sunday, they asked questions about where people are at, what makes them different, how we celebrate our difference as people created in the image of God (or if the worship leader would stop to ask what style of music people enjoy, or how they might better express their love for God and each other within new rituals)?

It is also liberating to think of normal people as experts. We are all experts on being who we are! You cannot, for example, ask a man to talk about being a woman. He may have a good idea, having related to women all his life, but the reality is that the ideas he holds are interpreted through his maleness. It is the same with other things, such as culture, sexuality, life stories and events, (dis)abilities, education and so on. All these things create differences, which historically have divided the church—first and foremost in terms of an us-and-them division between leaders and laity. Yet if we start to view the other person as an expert, it fosters respect and curiosity about who the person is and how they became who they are.

People often expect psychotherapists to tell them what to do, yet when we take a position of non-judgment and acknowledge that clients have the expertise of being who they are, they will make their own judgments, which they can own and which fit with their experiences. For Christians, to adopt such a position would help us to remain in relationship with people instead of taking the moral high ground and assuming that others should defer automatically to our beliefs—whether we find ourselves involved in a heavy counselling situation; or releasing a young person, who may not believe quite what I believe, to use her own unique musical talents within a church service; or simply chatting to a neighbour with whom we have differing views. Jesus' commission was to make disciples and not converts. We can do this through creating and merging new rituals that open up new possibilities and facilitate a recognition of our emerging selves and our relationship with God.

MOVING ON

Amid the possibilities that begin to open up, new metaphors and rituals emerge, which are owned and develop in meaning as they are actively shared within a 'system' (or community). When we first sought to re-contextualize an ancient Christian walking meditation called the Labyrinth within our worship community (*Live On Planet Earth*), it became a symbol of our own identity, a milestone on our journey. The rituals we created around it expressed our journey, who we had become. When we moved to London and shared the Labyrinth service with another alternative worship community, *Grace*, it became a part of their journey too, yet the rituals began to change—they expressed new things, expressed old and new stories. It also became impossible to know which elements were from *Live On Planet Earth* and which were from *Grace*. These rituals are now being shared with the wider church community, through St Paul's Cathedral, a cathedral tour, Youth for Christ and the Labyrinth kit.

This sharing can be both liberating and constraining. Sometimes we heard what had been done to the Labyrinth and wanted to weep. Aspects of our journey that we had invested with significance had been changed. But this, ultimately, prompted us to understand our need to discover and be curious about other groups' journeys, their understanding and meaning, which allows the differences to create a new thing not just for them, but for us and our own community.

A few months ago, I was asked by a close colleague what it was that I really believed in. I could see all my Christian friends clapping their hands with glee—at last, the opportunity to launch into a 'You-must-be-born-again' moment! Yet I was aware of the context from which my friend came: her spirituality (she is a practising Jew) should inform my response to her question. We had also other conversations in which she had stated that Jesus was a social construction to control people, which was an added factor that informed my response.

My response was simple, yet true. I stated that I knew that there were lots of different ways of thinking about Jesus (this acknowledged and validated her own viewpoint, and made way for my story to be heard). I then told her that the stories of Jesus create something very beautiful in my life; and the more I become like those stories, the more I seem able to love, to be honest, to share myself with people, to live life to the full. To this, she responded that she wanted that kind of spirituality, which opened up further opportunities for us both to discover about God from each other. Had I not known the context or used previous conversations to inform me, my response may have prevented us from being able to explore and share our spiritual journey together.

The conversation that took place has allowed us to share in the rituals our families perform. My family were welcome guests at her son's *bar mitzvah*, and, as a gift to her son, I am in the process of preparing a book with stories (both Christian and Jewish) about the process of becoming a man. In creating the book, I am not only participating in the ritual itself but I am also being allowed to create something new—stories in the form of a book that will be passed down from my friend's son to his son. The book itself will be a part of the ritual that will shape and inform future generations. It is sometimes in the witnessing of, and therefore participating in, a ritual that new life comes.

It often feels odd that Jesus bothered to mix spit in the mud and rub it into the blind man's eyes. It seems unhygienic and really rather pointless, when Jesus only needed to have said the word. Perhaps the point was that Jesus performed this ritual because he knew the man needed it in order to enter healing. How often, as the Church, have we marginalized others and excluded them from a relationship with God by going straight for the healing, rather than enabling people, through the co-creating of rituals, to make way for change, healing and 'w-holiness'?

Whether specifically in our 'worship times', or more widely as we begin to see our lives creatively as works of art, as expressions of worship within the relationships we inhabit, the time is right to create new possibilities, to open up dialogues, to ask questions and to dream new ways of being. Before we ask specifically how this might look, we should be asking what it means to be the people of God, what it means to live our lives as acts of worship, what others can teach us, what we have come to presume is true, what we can learn from the exciting new changes that are happening in 'the world'. Some of these simple techniques from the world of psychotherapy can help us to look at our lives, our relationships, our churches and our beliefs through fresh eyes. The possibilities are endless, the future an open book, a blank page, on which we can all begin to create new dreams—together.

EPILOGUE

Last year my parents returned to Ecuador, where they work as missionaries. This is the commissioning I wrote for their farewell service. I share it with you because in the sharing we can enter into our own commissioning.

My sister and I had letters that spelled the word 'grace'. We said the following as we gave my parents the letters.

We give you this G for Gender. God made man and woman in their own image. The Trinity God is a God of justice and equality, but also a God who celebrates difference with unity. We ask you to keep the Grace of God as you seek to empower men and women to reach their full potential.

We give you this R for Relationship. God the Trinity lives in perfect community and therefore relationship. We commission you to keep the gRace of God as you seek to relate to the people of Ecuador.

We give you this A for Action. God is a God who seeks to act in our lives and the lives of others, yet is a God who is gentle and compassionate, who never asks us to action without having been in the action first. We commission you to keep the grAce of God as you seek to bring God's action in people's lives.

We give you this C for Culture and Creativity. God created the diversity of culture, yet is beyond it. We commission you to keep the graCe for the people of Ecuador and we ask God to give you their creative energy to enable you to translate and enact the good news to a people who are diverse in culture.

We give you this E for Event. God is a God who knows past, present and future events. We commission you to keep the gracE and remember past events, move forward into future events and store this event in your heart.

The congregation then said:

We give you God's GRACE, not as an IKEA flatpack, but as a key that opens a whole new world of God-inspired possibilities. May the GRACE of our Lord Jesus Christ be with you now and always.

We concluded together:

May the GRACE of our Lord Jesus Christ and the love of God and the fellowship of the Holy Spirit be with us now and always. Amen.

DEEP CURRENTS OF THE HEART

Mike Riddell

A few years ago, I went to see an exhibition by a New Zealand artist named Ralph Hotere, who lives in my home town of Dunedin. Ralph is renowned for working with impenetrable blackness, and for the use of his art as a form of protest. Some of the work shown included window-frames containing glass that had been painted black. As you peered into the window, there was nothing to be seen—until eventually you became aware of your own reflection staring back at you, scanning you for meaning. It was disconcerting. That which should be transparent had instead become self-revealing.

But the piece that took my breath away was entitled 'Black Phoenix'. It was a large installation work, which had been given an entire room of the gallery to itself. Emerging from the wall was the prow of a fishing boat, with all of the timber blackened by fire. Hotere had salvaged it from an inferno at a boat-builder's yard. The artwork was surrounded by long lengths of fire-ravaged timber, sections of which had been machined back to reveal the warmth and grain of the wood. The effect was overpowering. It almost knocked me to the floor, literally. I stayed in the room for a long time, walking around, squatting, contemplating.

It was a visual symphony of irrepressible life in the context of death. The boat burst through the wall with monumental vitality—ravaged by fire, blackened and scarred, seared and baptized with flame; yet it crested the wave of death and thundered relentlessly into the oceans of possibility. The surrounding timbers with their incisions revealed that the fire had scoured the surface but not penetrated to the depths. Underneath the seeming annihilation, there was life and beauty. 'Death cannot conquer life,' the work proclaimed. Surging out of the flames, the tortured craft carried with it all the dignity, suffering and hope of human existence.

This was resurrection broken out of verbal confines, bludgeoning the imagination and challenging any resistance. No sermon I have ever heard has approached the power or lingering effect of that artwork. Here was no abstract discussion of rumours of immortality; this was immediate, visceral and inescapable. I was broken open by it, and left overwhelmed and exhausted. It was a religious experience, in the deepest sense of the term. How is it, I pondered later, that I had been moved at this level by an encounter entirely devoid of explicit content? Why should the burnt-out hulk of a fishing vessel evoke such deep meditations on mortality?

I fancy the answer lies somewhere between Jung and Tillich, with both of them prospecting in the vicinity of the same vein of experience. Jung might point to the title of the artwork, 'Black Phoenix', and speak of its archetypal resonance. Lurking within our unconscious are ancient cyphers, freighted with generations of significance and psychic power. Death, resurrection, fire of purgation—these are monsters of the deep, brought to the surface by Hotere's artistic net. It was not the installation itself that caused me to tremble, but rather the archetypes that it unleashed in my imagination. Jung might understand this as the proper role of art, dredging into the substratum of the inner world.

Tillich would prefer the terminology of symbols. That great burnt bulk of the boat exploding into the gallery is a symbol. As such, it does not simply 'signify' something (as a sign would do), but participates in a reality that it mediates to the observer. The function of the symbol, according to Tillich, is to open the human soul to those verities that cannot be communicated in any other way. At depth, the symbol is sluicing a pathway to ultimate reality, or 'the ground of being', which is the category of transcendence. I found the experience in the gallery to be religious because it was: through the power of symbol I was touching that which is holy. Beyond rational apprehension and material life, there is the realm of the ultimate, which occasionally punctures it.

Jung and Tillich agree on two things that I wish to develop. The first is that the power of both art and religion is 'at depth'. When we discuss ritual or symbol or sacrament, we are touching upon the deep currents of the heart. This is an ocean of primal experience where words often fail. I commented some years ago that in my own experience of writing fiction, the inspiration came 'from the dark vaults of imagination where rationality and ethical thinking are at a low ebb'. It is the realm where dreams are forged, demons are active and God speaks. We quite properly fear it, and use various devices to keep our distance from it in the course of ordinary life. But that is not to diminish its existence, as many failed secularists have discovered.

The second point of consensus is that archetypal or symbolic activity is universal in human experience. Not only does it cross the boundaries of all religious traditions but is capable of operating independently of them. No framework of faith at all is necessary to be moved by an artwork such as 'Black Phoenix', or to be terrified by a disturbing dream. The capacity is given in and with human existence. This is to say that human life is open at its core level to experiencing a dimension that lies well below the surface of common perception. Artists, priests and psychotherapists know this instinctively, and would not be able to work without making use of the fact. We are inescapably religious creatures.

A regular feature of alternative worship groups around the world has been that of the Labyrinth, which is sometimes described as 'walking prayer'. In its most basic form, it consists of a spiral path drawn on the floor, which pilgrims move along until they reach the centre, after which they retrace their steps. Many people testify to the way in which their participation in this simple activity becomes a sacred event. Some speak of meeting God in the process. It is not, of course, a specifically Christian pursuit. The Labyrinth has its origins in pagan times, and today is celebrated in many different 'new age' contexts. But for many who walk it, it seems to have the capacity to bring them into touch with the transcendent.

It is an activity suffused with association. The connection between walking and pilgrimage is very old in human history. The design of a labyrinth is circular, and spiralling in towards the centre is akin to re-entering the womb (which Jesus told us was not possible). The space in the middle where participants rest has both a meditative and sexual energy, and is probably charged with both. All of these connotations contribute to the way in which the Labyrinth is experienced, and go a certain way to explaining its effect. It becomes a way of mediating spiritual encounter, while being non-specific in meaning. This, I suspect, is true of ritual in general.

The Dunedin group with which I have been associated, *Soul Outpost*, has regularly hosted Labyrinths. They have attracted people from many backgrounds, including a Buddhist meditation group that promoted it among their members. We fell into the habit of providing the elements of communion at such occasions. Off to one side, a low table was situated with a candle burning, together with bread and a cup of wine. We made no comment about these elements, nor gave any direction in regard to them, yet I cannot think of anyone who participated in the

Labyrinth who did not also afterwards kneel at that table to eat and drink.

There is no way of knowing what meaning they ascribed to it. I suspect that, if questioned, those without Christian faith would have been quite inarticulate in explaining their participation in what is the central Christian ritual—but it would have meant something to them. The sacralized activity has a power in and of itself, which does not require explanation or framework of faith to be effective. How could it be otherwise, when it has lain at the heart of Western culture for at least 1500 years? We did not kid ourselves that, by participating in this ceremony, those involved had somehow been Christianized, and we were conscious of violating church protocols in the way this quasi-eucharist was offered, but in this age of clashing symbols it seemed appropriate.

All of this is by way of saying that when we discuss ritual, we are talking about something much broader and deeper than the subset of Christian ritual. It is innate human behaviour, as primitive and as potent as the sexual act. Ritual exists, I suspect, as a means of protection for the human species. The realm of the ultimate cannot possibly be digested or encountered in raw form, and 'anyone who sees God's face will die' (Exodus 33:20, CEV). The forces that operate in the world of archetypes, or what we might paraphrase as the ground zero of being, are simply overwhelming. Allowed to flow untrammelled into human consciousness, they produce either madness or dissolution.

In my country, we still have active volcanoes. One in particular has been troublesome of late, with spills of volcanic debris escaping from the crater lake and causing damage as they pour down the mountainside. Recently, major earthworks have been completed to erect barriers and dig channels for any further overflows. They will act to direct the spills in certain directions. Rituals are something like this. They are ditches dug into experience to channel the molten lava of the holy, allowing it to flow without causing havoc. Only through this safety device are we enabled to live anywhere in the vicinity of the volcano.

Even so, rituals themselves are potent. Just because lava flows in a prescribed channel, that doesn't mean it is safe. All cultures and faiths have recognized this, and sought to provide further safeguards. Rituals are generally surrounded by an elaborate interpretative context, which is the equivalent of building fences alongside the channels of fire. Such explanations limit the reach and potency of the ritual, and help to prevent damage. Usually there is further control exercised by appointing recognized guardians of the rituals, who undergo preparation in order to administer them on behalf of the community. In this way the ceremonies are regulated and the dangers minimized.

Within the Christian framework, we have the category of sacraments. These are the central rituals of the church, mediating, it is said, the very being of God. The usual protective measures are invoked. Theological reflection and church order combine to establish quite precisely the meaning and function of each ritual. They prescribe the range of meanings that are allowed, and the range that are prohibited. And we hardly need to mention the licensed functionaries who closely control administration of and access to the sacraments. It may well be that the entire concept of the clergy has been generated in response to a perceived need to regulate such activities.

I would not want to decry the accumulated wisdom of millennia of human history, which has recognized the potential perils associated with tapping deep wells and moved to limit the damage. But this is an age of deconstruction and decentring, and it may be a time to reassess our attitude to ritual. A ritual is itself a protective measure; do we need further protections? The sophisticated barriers erected by the church seem to be similar in character to what the Jewish faith called 'fencing the Law', which resulted in the numerous prohibitions of Pharisaism denounced by Jesus. They produce a distancing of people from God and from themselves—a tempering of raw experience which is safer but ultimately less satisfying.

When I go to Mass, I am not interested any more in understanding what it means. I am a little suspicious of any interpretations at all. I want to stumble to the front to eat and drink, and then kneel in quietness with the warmth of the wine radiating in my belly and the residue of wafer still clinging to the roof of my mouth. There is something going on there, but I dare not name it. The priests and theologians may feel they have a handle on it, but I think they are mistaken. I sometimes look at the faces of the people in the ragged queue advancing up the aisle. What I see there is a hunger for participation in mystery, not a quest for understanding.

In my first novel, *The Insatiable Moon*,[60] I made an attempt at describing a midweek communion in an Anglican church. I described the handful of parishioners present as follows:

Shuffling to the front to kneel at the rail. Opening their mouths like goldfish to cannibalise their God. It's the eating and the drinking, the tasting and the smelling. God's so bloody ephemeral, so wispy, so hard to get hold of amidst tangibles like cancer and divorce. Too big or too small, it doesn't matter which. God in the pure sense is untouchable, and so useless. Here you have him in a form you can grapple with. Fit him in your mouth, swallow him, digest him in your stomach. The physical taste of God—it's something you can get a liking for.

Not entirely orthodox, but a possible reading of the event.

I'm not sure whether the Church's zeal for her rituals is to protect God from the masses or to protect the masses from God, but a large part of this caution is unwarranted and counter-productive to any notion of mission. Forgive me for wishing there were a lot more unprotected sacral activity in church. But to focus on the sacraments of Christianity is to fall into the bad habits of Christendom and view the rest of humanity as 'outsiders'. The universal existence of ritual in all ages and cultures is evidence that people everywhere seek to engage those mysteries of life that are to be found at depth. Christians have no monopoly on the holy.

Whatever religious authorities may think of the development, we live in a time when the ritual has been liberated. Once confined to the administration of institutions or coherent communities, rituals have been set free to roam uncharted territories. Not only have the people at large felt free to plunder ceremonies from wherever they will—witness the cooption of Native American 'sweatlodges', or the revival of Druid practices—but they have begun to create their own. There are blessing circles, menstruation rites, fire-dances and samhain liturgies. Psychotherapists, dance instructors or self-proclaimed shamans are as likely to lead such rituals as any cleric.

This is all part of the democratization of faith—a breaking out of enthusiasm for DIY religion. It is a symptom of the historic separation of spirituality from religious institutions. Not surprisingly, the heady freedom that comes from the recognition that people can organize their own sacramental life has produced some very silly results, but excess is always the companion of liberty. Personally I welcome the dangerous unshackling of spiritual exploration from the neurotic control mechanisms that stifled it. With it has come the recognition that the province of organized religion is a very small valley in the planet of human experience—and the lava, which was beginning to cool and solidify, has begun to flow again.

For Christianity, it represents a call to re-engage with humanity. There are two obvious ways in which we can adapt our attitude to rituals in response to that call. The first is to make our own rites public once more. In my experience, baptism is a much more potent event when performed in a public space, and I have participated in several eucharists that took place as an act of both celebration and protest under the curious gaze of onlookers. The crucifixion of Christ, after all, did not take place in some dimly lit and carpeted sanctuary. On one memorable occasion, in connection with protests against South African apartheid, a large cross was confiscated by police as an offensive weapon. Better that than having it adopted as a fashion accessory.

The second response would be to participate in rituals that have meaning outside of the faith community. To do so is not a betrayal of our core beliefs, but rather a deep appreciation of the central mystery of our faith, which is that of incarnation. Through Christ, it seems to me, we understand the general nature of reality, which is that it is saturated in divine potential. This is not the pantheistic view that everything is at root God, but that the nature of creation is such that any element of it may become a symbol in the Tillichian sense—a mediator of the presence and activity of God. Human experience is a common vehicle of revelation, and not just for those who count themselves sanctified.

Ritual is a means of exposing the sacral depths of life. Traditionally for the church, the points of intersection with common culture have been those of baptism, marriage and death. In an age when these ceremonies are subject to a takeover bid by secular 'celebrants', it is important for the church to recognize the missiological significance of such events. I have attended funerals where the priest seemed to be enduring a slightly distasteful but necessary routine, akin to doing the dishes—this at the major transition point of human life, when mortality and the meaning of existence come into view for all participants. Often in ignorance we pass up what is a unique opportunity not to preach a sermon, but, like Jesus at Cana, to join in and facilitate the celebration of major turning points of life.

But more than this, there are a host of other opportunities for involvement in those times that ordinary people regard as 'special'. I have participated in house blessings, naming ceremonies, factory dedications and even a rather dubious liturgy for the launching of a boat. In this I have no doubt learned from the Maori influence in New Zealand, where the *tohanga* (holy person) is present wherever the people are, providing prayers and ceremonies for the very stuff of life. I understand that this has also been a feature of the Celtic approach to soaking the ordinary in wonder. The role of the priest is surely not to impose meaning on people, but to help them to uncover and contemplate the meaning that is already present.

Such a function is not, of course, the preserve of clergy. It is an attitude to life that may be adopted by all the people of faith. Despite ridicule, my family persists in holding hands and making some expression of thanks at every meal eaten around the table. I find it a simple but important recognition of the sacrality of people, food and conversation. Communal celebrations such as birthdays, graduations, farewells and house-warmings are not distractions from religion but the essence of it. Christ is to be found among the people, not off in some corner despising them. In these confusing times, many are at a loss to know how to signify transition appropriately other than by getting drunk. The people perish for want of a ritual. Let us provide them with one.

It is not the specific nature of a particular ritual which is the difficult part of responding to contemporary culture. Various symbolic actions will suggest themselves, whether they involve the cutting of string, the burning of relics of the past, the planting of a tree, the washing of water, the casting of stones into a pool or the recitation of a poem. The key is not the specific channel chosen to carry the deep currents of the heart, but the attitude that recognizes the necessity of doing so. Only when we understand that all of human life is sacred and of religious significance will we shape our rituals to meet it. The history of Christianity in filling pagan festivals with new meaning suggests that our forebears understood that their faith was about fulfilment rather than annihilation.

A few years ago, I took part in a worship service at Greenbelt where the theme was given as 'Heaven on earth'. As part of it, I introduced a ritual which I called the sacrament of the peanut. Large bowls of unshelled peanuts were passed among people, and they were invited to take some and eat them. I introduced the ritual by saying I had no idea what it meant, but that I had a gut feeling it was connected to our theme. That much was true; I had only the instinct that there was something about concealment, interiority and the necessity of peeling away the surface to get at the nut which might be appropriate. Judging by the conversations that followed, many people infused the rite with their own meaning, and so it became a genuine vehicle of encounter for them.

The fact is that life is ambiguous, and help is often needed to uncover the 'nut' of mystery that is hidden in every dull moment. Our major Christian sacrament finds awe in bread and wine, the staples of existence. This should engender an orientation that makes us delve into every part of common life, digging like prospectors for that gleam of gold. Through provision of and participation in the people's ritual, we allow the divine to shine and bless all with revealing light. To undertake this requires both a physical and theological relocation of the church, so that she might abandon her geographic and cultural ghetto. Christ is risen for all humanity, and we dare not seek to keep him from his people.

Artists are our allies in this regard. For millennia, they have sought to channel the raw magma of existence to a population that is often content to get on with things, oblivious to how thin is the crust on which they stand. This is an age for both encouraging the artists among us and for learning from their craft. No artist worth their salt is promoting a message in their work or attempting to convince people of anything. Rather, like Hotere, they are providing windows into the undergirding mystery, which is allowed to speak for itself. The artwork is effective in direct proportion to its ability to act as a conductor for those deep and dangerous currents of the heart. Perhaps the church could provide fewer placards and more windows.

If we can overcome our neurotic need to explain and regulate, the church's long experience with ritual and symbol might stand us in good stead to become spiritual midwives. We of all people should be equipped to understand how deep is the amalgam of spirit and flesh of which the creation story speaks. Humanity bears the kiss and breath of God, and no life can be regarded as ordinary any more. The population at large may suffer amnesia or wilful ignorance of this fact, but memories and relics abide in the subterranean chambers of consciousness. Some of the old pathways to the surface may be blocked and others destroyed. It is our job, quite simply, to open them again; and to get out of the way.

RITUAL AS STRATEGIC PRACTICE

Jonny Baker

A TURN TOWARDS RITUAL

In the Western Church there is currently a turn towards ritual. Some denominations or traditions will claim that they never turned away from it—which may be true, and we are grateful to them for their faithful preservation of the gifts that they have stewarded. But even those low church groups for whom ritual and being ritualistic was part of what they wanted to get away from, in their search for new freedom of expression in worship, are changing their tune. It is increasingly common to find candle lighting, symbolic embodied acts, icons, greater attention to ritual space, stations of the cross, anointing with oil, the laying on of hands, labyrinth walking, eucharistic practice and the introduction of liturgy in charismatic and evangelical circles. Youth ministry is beginning to make a similar journey as it struggles to move its focus away from entertainment to spiritual encounter.

Alternative worship groups have played a significant part in leading the way in this area, with their re-appropriation of many old rituals, often giving them their own contemporary take, and with their invention of several new ones. In *Grace*,[61] we have certainly discovered ritual as a powerful means of choreographing a multi-sensory embodied encounter with God. God meets us in ritual, so we nearly always try to incorporate some sort of ritual in which everybody is involved. It opens up a window in the soul and the community through which the breeze of the Spirit can blow. It seems to draw a service together and seal what has taken place. It helps move worship from the head to the heart.

Ritual is being rediscovered as a wonderful gift and resource that can have a real quality and depth that resonates in our own particular cultural situation. This is also mirrored in the wider culture where there has been an explosion of interest in all forms of spirituality, including ritual.

THINKING ABOUT RITUAL

The notion of ritual first emerged as a formal term of analysis in the 19th century. Thinking about ritual has mainly been located in cultural anthropology, often trying to make sense of the meaning of rituals of particular tribal groups or ancient cultures. Ritual Studies has now become an academic discipline in its own right (albeit relatively new), focusing on ritual at home as well as in other cultures. It has a lot of insights to help us reflect on the current turn towards ritual.

These are some of the current emphases in Ritual Studies:

- **Not a universal phenomenon:** The attempts of earlier studies to find what universally defines ritual, to come up with a grand theory that explains it, have been rejected. 'Ritual is not a universal cross-cultural phenomenon but a particular way of looking at and organising the world that tells us as much about the anthropologist and his or her frame of reference as the people or behaviour being studied.'[62] There has been an increased tendency to focus on a specific context, being concerned with 'the native point of view'.

- **Dynamic, not rigid:** Ritual was once conceived of as formal, traditional and unchanging, with routine as its hallmark. While it is still recognized that it can be these things, there is much greater emphasis on the dynamic nature of ritual and its capacity to be experimental, subversive and counter-cultural. Rites can be invented, individual, new.

- **Symbols, not words:** Whereas earlier studies tended to give primacy to words, there is now much more emphasis on symbols and the cultural system of meaning within which they are embedded. The symbols used need to communicate by connecting with the cultural world of participants for ritual to be effective.

- **Embodied:** There is a tendency to focus on ritual's experiential, performative, physical, bodily and gestural features. Bocock suggests that 'the use of the body, together with visual and aural symbols, places ritual at the centre of attention if our concern is with the split in our culture between the body and the mind: the non-rational and the over rational'.[63] Earlier theorists' analyses are criticized for emphasizing cognitive and verbal aspects, to the virtual exclusion of emotions. Part of the appeal of theories of performance is the heightened multi-sensory experiences they afford to the whole embodied person.

- Transforming: Ritual has a role in the transformation of society and individuals. Earlier theories posited a simple mirroring of society and culture, but it is now recognized that ritual is both generated by and generative of society and culture. 'Ritual is constitutive of experience since it transforms the experiential base out of which people live their everyday lives.'[64]

- Fashionable: Presently, ritual is a fashionable idea. This is so both in the academic world and also in people's everyday lives. 'Ritual has become a counter-cultural fad, the object of rampant experientialism, that is the belief that experience per se is authoritative.'[65] In spite of a decline in interest in institutional forms of ritual, the need for ritual and the practice of ritual have not declined. Rather, they have intensified and increased as institutionalized forms have lost their appeal and effectiveness.

- Open to the sacred: While institutional religion has declined, there has also been a resurgence of interest in spirituality. Ritual is seen by many as a 'window open on one side to the eternal'.[66] In many discussions 'spirituality' and 'the sacred' are fairly vague notions but there is nonetheless a hunger to encounter something divine, whether by turning inwards or outwards.

RITUAL AS PRACTICE

One of the best contemporary scholars in Ritual Studies is Catherine Bell. In her book *Ritual Theory, Ritual Practice*,[67] she managed to redraw the map, or at least throw down the gauntlet to cultural interpretations of ritual, reconceiving a different way of thinking about ritual as strategic practice. She draws from practice theory, in particular the work of Pierre Bourdieu.[68]

Practice is an irreducible term for human activity. Its concern is with how people make a life—that is, how they actually live in practice on a day-to-day basis. Bell highlights four features of practice—that it is (a) situational; (b) strategic; (c) embedded in a misrecognition of what it is, in fact, doing; and (d) able to reconfigure a vision of the order of power in the world, or 'redemptive hegemony'. I will consider the current turn towards ritual through three of these four features.[69]

Situational: consumption and changing religious practice

First, to say that human activity is situational is to recognize that what is important about it cannot be grasped outside its immediate context. What, then, are some of the contours of the current context in which there is a turn towards ritual?

The standard theory used to make sense of religion since the 1950s has been secularization. Its story says that the Western world is in an advanced state of living without gods and its society runs on non-religious principles. It is inhospitable to faith, religion and the sacred. Church attendance and social influence declines and religion becomes increasingly marginal to society at large. On the surface, this seems to be a tenable theory. Certainly in the UK, Christian churches, particularly the main denominations, are only too painfully aware of their waning influence and the decline in church attendance over the last 20 years, especially among the young.[70] In recent years, however, much to the surprise of some commentators, there has been an explosion of interest in spirituality—but this is not doing anything to affect the decline in numbers attending churches. The majority of these spiritual explorers don't connect their personal quest with the church.

Why is it that so few people who are searching for spiritual meaning either look for it or find it in the institutional church? Several writers have concluded that the church has so wedded itself to the culture of modernity that modernity is the only frame of reference in which it knows how to operate. The institutional church is assumed to be part of the old order that has failed. Going to church feels like visiting another era. This is seen in the cerebral nature of expressions of faith, emphasis on doctrines, propositional truth, the pervasive rationalism, and the old-fashioned patriarchy that still seems so evident.

While elsewhere in the culture there is a fascination with mystery, the numinous, angels, heaven and the after-life, 'at best the church seems to speak uncomfortably about them'.[71] Postmodern times are tactile, symbolic and image-based, while in the church it's still words, words and more words. Those best touched by the intuitive, artistic and creative find little that speaks to them in church. Postmodern times elevate experience, community and ritual, but the ritual on offer in churches somehow feels empty and boring. It's what Scheff calls 'overdistancing'[72]—that is, it has an absence of emotion. Postmodern times celebrate the body and being human. The dualism in much of the theology of the church has left a view of bodies and matter as bad, and this in turn has been destructive of ritual. Because of this, when people do look to Christian rituals, they find ritual action that often contradicts their own basic feelings. This is all compounded by a general failure to take postmodern times and, in particular, people's spiritual search seriously.

Another aspect of the current situation is that Western culture now runs under the logic of consumption. Shopping has become all-consuming—the lens through which all of life is approached and negotiated, including religious life. This consumer culture is facilitated by the growth of communication and information technologies and new media whose impact cannot be underestimated.[73] Social interaction and organization take on a new cultural pattern. People find and construct meaning routes through everyday life to help them negotiate the terrain, and these routes are no longer simply defined by tradition, family or geography. The range of choices confronting people is immense. In part, they negotiate meaning in society via networks and relationships and the construction of identity (or identities). Both are related. Identity is increasingly seen as something constructed via taste and selective consumption, and is used to make distinctions from others. The networks of relationships are often those from whom approval is sought through similar lifestyle and tastes.

The flows of information round these networks are increasing aided by the technologies, and the whole process seems to be very fluid and changing. Usually they have some location in place, but not necessarily and certainly not exclusively. Culture is increasingly fragmented and there are a range of worldviews, meanings, lifestyles and subcultures at play. Culture is, in this sense, a 'site for contested meanings' within which people find manifold ways of living the practice of everyday life.

Zygmunt Bauman is wonderfully evocative and perceptive in his descriptions of people's 'life strategies' in postmodern times. One of the themes he returns to time and again is the construction of identity. He contrasts modern and postmodern approaches to identity, concluding that 'the hub of postmodern life strategy is not identity building but the avoidance of being fixed'.[74] He sees the 'pilgrim' as an appropriate allegory for identity-building under the conditions of modernity. The pilgrim knows where he or she is going, weaves each event or site of pilgrimage into a coherent 'sense-making story' and is living with a purpose of fulfilment. The 'tourist' is the most appropriate metaphor to describe postmodern life strategy. avoiding being fixed. The tourist avoids being fixed: he or she is a systematic seeker of new and different experiences, but needs to keep moving, travelling light. Relationships with locals are likely to be skin-deep and mustn't tie the tourist down. The tourist must be able to get up and move on and shake off the experience whenever they wish.

The implications for religious practice are enormous. In this new world, religious practice has been and still is rapidly changing. Lyon suggests that within a consumer culture, religion is best viewed as a dynamic cultural resource rather than an organizational form or fixed entity.[75] This certainly seems to be the way a lot of individuals and groups treat it, though I suspect it would be one resisted by the guardians of declining religious institutions. The new explosion of spirituality described above is easily dismissed by them, precisely because it seems to be reflective of consumerist attitudes and lifestyles. But if consumption is the way people make sense of life, then isn't this precisely where we should expect to find openings for religious activity?

This is not to say that there isn't much about a consumer culture that needs to be resisted and challenged. Once people connect with a Christian community, the challenge to see discipleship as a lifelong commitment rather than another consumer choice will be an important and difficult one. But the point is that religious life in postmodern times has not dried up as predicted by the theorists; it is being relocated. Patterns of religious behaviour are being restructured. This includes the way many Christians now approach their faith and church. As an example of this, a recent survey of people who have left church[76] shows that people who were once committed members of churches are now weaving meaningful religious experience and community into their lives in new patterns. People's relationship to Greenbelt, Taizé, Internet sites and communities is also already functioning in this way. This kind of new spiritual practice is invisible to many institutions and to their accounts of and ways of measuring religious life in the world. I suspect that this will be an increasing trend. People will increasingly connect with churches and institutions only if there is seen to be something worth connecting with— a depth of spirituality and experience, something real, the possibility of encounter with God, genuine community.

Some of the considerations of 'situation', then, for ritual practice are that it is located, in postmodern times, in a time of increased hunger for spirituality but decline in institutional religion. Situated in a time when consumption has moved to centre stage, there are pilgrims who will be looking to make some meaningful connection between rituals and their life story, and tourists who will have the experience and try to move on. Both may be treating ritual practice (and religion) as a cultural resource to weave into the meaning routes they construct through life.

Strategic: ritual and everyday life

To recognize that practice is strategic is to see that it employs schemes and tactics to improvise and negotiate through everyday situations. De Certeau's classic *The Practice of Everyday Life* focuses on the tactical nature of everyday practices of consumers. He particularly points out the many and varied ways of 'making do' that subvert the dominant systems in which people live.

One of the problems with worship in the church is its dislocation from the rest of life. This is what people mean when they describe church as irrelevant. One of the moves made in alternative worship has been to try to remove this dislocation by bringing the real world into church and taking church back into the real world. This includes the choreographing of ritual space, the use of popular culture and images, the tone of language, the reframing of traditions, rethinking of theology and so on. Something as simple as having a communion service informally in people's homes around the meal table can make new connections. The use of a music track in worship may enable it to be heard differently the next time it is on the radio.

In *Grace* we recently did a service for Lent, exploring the idea of desert. In discussion while planning the service, we agreed that no one in the group (which is based in London) was likely to go to an actual desert, so we considered what might be a contemporary equivalent of desert in the city. Someone suggested that the closest most people come to solitude is being stuck in a traffic jam. Part of the service involved visiting a series of stations in the ritual space. We took this idea of a traffic jam as a contemporary experience of solitude for one of the stations. We videoed a journey in the car in London, projected this image on to a screen and placed a row of chairs facing the screen. We then recorded a CD of instrumental music which we labelled 'Grace traffic-island discs' and placed a CD Walkman with headphones on each chair. The ritual consisted of sitting in a chair, staring at a traffic jam, listening to music. It was very amusing to watch! But the strategy behind this kind of move is that the next time someone who participated in the ritual is stuck in a traffic jam, there is the possibility that it will be reframed for them as a moment of solitude in which to pray or be still or listen to a spiritual piece of music.

This does no less than transform people, enabling them to see the world and act in it in a new way; at least, it has the potential to do so. Catherine Bell's language for it (which takes some getting used to) would be that it creates a ritualized agent, an actor with a form of ritual mastery, 'who embodies flexible sets of cultural schemes and can deploy them effectively in multiple situations so as to restructure those situations in practical ways'.[77] So, to take another example, to walk the Labyrinth is to enter ritual space. The whole person, the ritual body, interacts with this environment. The act of walking slowly round the Labyrinth with God, rather than the usual rushing along in urban life, doesn't merely communicate the need to slow down. It generates a slowed-down person aware of God's presence in life. The simple act of dropping a stone in water to let go of pressures and concerns at the 'letting go' station of the Labyrinth[78] does not merely communicate the need to let go. It produces a person freed from pressure in and through the act itself. It is in this sense that the Labyrinth walker is a 'ritualized agent'.

Ritual mastery is the way in which schemes deployed in the Labyrinth can then be used in a variety of circumstances beyond the rite itself. In the 'self' station, the walker stops to hear some verses from Psalm 139, affirming their uniqueness, as they look in a mirror. The next time they look in a mirror, they may well see themselves in a new way. The connection with ordinary everyday things is strategic. One priest on duty in St Paul's Cathedral, who walked the Labyrinth, described the lingering impression of the video image of a flickering soundline at the 'noise' station and how he had been reflecting on it since. He had deployed this scheme of the Labyrinth back into the circumstances of his life. This can be very empowering for participants. Many have described it using the words 'a powerful experience'. Bell seems to subscribe this transforming effect to the process of ritualization itself, but from a theological point of view, as well as recognizing the power of ritualization, the transforming effect is more than just a constructed experience. It is also affected by the Holy Spirit of God, whose presence is real, albeit that the sacred comes to us cloaked in cultural forms.

Redemptive hegemony: ritual and tradition

Hegemony[79] recognizes the system of power relations in a society. Redemptive process describes the way people can act within the system of power so that the power relations are reproduced and people have a sense of their place within them, but can still negotiate space to act within that in ways that are empowering for them. So, saying that practice is able to reconfigure a vision of the order of power within the world (redemptive hegemony) is to recognize that practice negotiates the existing power relations in such a way as to empower individuals within it, but without their either leaving or destroying the system. I have already considered the way in which ritual can be empowering for individuals. Here I want to consider how the practice of ritual can be a strategic way of renewing tradition.

In postmodern times, when so little seems fixed and everything is in flux, tradition and continuity actually offer a sense of weight of history, an anchor point. The Christian tradition has two thousand years of history, building on a previous four thousand years or so of history before that which it shares with the Jews. It's a tradition with a huge global network, diversity, examples and stories of ways in which the church has passed on the dangerous memory of Jesus, a catalogue of mistakes made and recovered from, and a wealth of spiritual resources. But far from being unchanging and fixed with a static set of 'cosmic symbols', it has been and is a living tradition. There are symbols (for example, the cross, bread and wine) that have been passed down for thousands of years, but there are also a whole range of new symbols and reinterpreted old symbols, such as the Labyrinth.

The use of tradition to claim that things must remain the same is, in that sense, not faithful to tradition at all; it is rather a dead traditionalism.

The tradition has to be struggled with and reformed to be carried forward. To keep reforming religious tradition in a prophetic spirit is to be faithful. It is from within the tradition itself that the tools and resources come to liberate people from the way tradition has been used to oppress them. So the injustices and inadequacies of a religious tradition are subverted paradoxically by the resources from within the tradition itself.[80]

It is commonly assumed that ritual is used to maintain a rigid and dogmatic tradition. Victor Turner, a well-known figure in Ritual Studies, grew disenchanted with this notion of ritual and developed a theory of ritual as both structure and anti-structure.[81] Rather than ritual being seen just as maintaining social control (structure), Turner introduced the notion that ritual as anti-structure could be subversive of structure and the status quo. Anti-ritualists often arise because of a view of ritual as structure (and then invent their own new rituals, even if they don't recognize them as such!), but they are in danger of losing or ignoring the weight of history. One of the discoveries of alternative worship groups has been that the resources to reinvigorate tradition and make it live within postmodern times lie within history and tradition, and not just within contemporary culture. Further, within tradition, the use of ritual can be a particularly effective means of mediating tradition and change—that is, appropriating some changes while maintaining a sense of cultural continuity.

One of the reasons for this is that ritual, even if relatively new and invented, has the semblance of having been passed down from previous generations. The appropriation of ritual by alternative worship groups is highly strategic in this sense. To give one example, *Grace* has developed several eucharistic prayers that are used in the ritual in much the same way as one of the officially sanctioned Anglican prayers. The theological take of one of these prayers is on the theme of hospitality, stressing Christ's open invitation to outsiders to share his table. If this was in a sermon, it could be thought of as someone's opinion, but in the heart of the eucharist it seems to carry much more power and weight. It is, in fact, a highly subversive text, raising questions about the church's practice of excluding certain groups of people from sharing the bread and wine. But as a ritual form, it is a very effective medium for change, while maintaining a sense of continuity. 'Whether it is being performed for the first time or the thousandth, the circumstance of being put in the ritual form gives something the effect of tradition.'[82]

THE CHALLENGE

The single most important challenge the church faces in the Western world is how to relate the Christian faith to a culture that runs under the logic of consumption. Bosch has shown well how, in different eras, there have been different tellings of the gospel.[83] We have to find ways in which the Christian faith is contextualized within our own cultural situation. This is always a risky task, but the possibility of the gospel outside of culture isn't an option available to us. Many of the practices of the Church are wedded to a bygone era. Old ways of doing evangelism and worship feel tired and are no longer working. An approach based on persuading people of the truth of Christianity's claims is no longer answering the questions they are asking. In a culture swamped with advertising, we've had enough sales pitches. Those who claim to know all the answers are viewed with suspicion.

The church should reshape its practice to connect with the genuine search for spiritual experience and encounter in our culture at the moment. The construction of genuine, meaningful, dynamic, multisensory, embodied rituals, both old and new, in church and out in the marketplace is an important part of that process.

Text, authority and ritual in the Church of England

1   In this sense, the National Lottery is a classic 'individual' ritual, performed by millions in their own time and own way, all culminating in an event watched by those millions to see if they have won. What such a ritual 'says' about the aims and aspirations of British society is another thing altogether.

2   Frank Senn, *New Creation*, Fortress Press, 2000, p. 136.

3   Senn, *New Creation*, p. 136.

4   For a quick treatment of ritual, see 'Rite' in J.G. Davies (ed.), *A New Dictionary of Liturgy and Worship*, SCM Press, 1986. For rites of passage, see A. van Gennep, *The Rites of Passage*, University of Chicago Press, 1961.

5   Alternative worship may mean different things in different cultures. What we am referring to here is a specific movement that developed in the UK to develop worship in ways that inculturated worship in contemporary culture, using dance music, images and rituals. For a good introduction to the movement, see www.alternativeworship.org.

6   See *Common Worship: Pastoral Services*, Church House Publishing, 2001, especially the Introduction, pp. 3–6.

7   *Pastoral Services*, p. 3.

8   *Pastoral Services*, p. 292.

The art of liturgy

9   Gregory Dix, *The Shape of the Liturgy* (2nd edn), Dacre, 1945, p. 710.

10 For instance, churches that belong to the Vineyard, New Frontiers or Pioneer networks.

11 I have borrowed this term from Wainwright (see note 12).

12 A. Jamieson, *A Churchless Faith*, SPCK, 2002, pp. 142–43.

13 J.A. Jungmann, *Pastoral Liturgy*, Challoner, 1962, pp. 80–89.

14 G. Wainwright, 'The Periods of Liturgical History', in Jones, Wainwright, Yarnold SJ and Bradshaw, *The Study of Liturgy*, SPCK, 1992, p. 65.

15 Milner White based his service on an earlier service from Truro Cathedral.

16 By Bryn and Sally Haworth, copyright © Bella Music Ltd.

Personalized ritual

17 Paul Roberts, *Alternative Worship and the Church of England*, Grove Books, 1999, p. 16.

18 Leonardo Boff, *Sacraments of Life, Life of Sacraments*, The Pastoral Press, 1987.

19 Catherine Bell, *Ritual: Perspectives and Dimensions*, Oxford University Press, 1997.

Black styles, rituals and mission for the 21st century

20 See Robert Beckford, *Dread and Pentecostal*, SPCK, 2000.

21 Kwesi Owusu (ed.), *Black British Culture and Society: A Text Reader*, Routledge, pp. 21–36.

22 Tony Sewell, *Black Masculinities and Schooling*, Trentham, 1997.

23 See Robert Beckford, *Jesus is Dread*, Darton, Longman & Todd, 1998.

24 See my previous work in *Growing into Hope: Believing and Expecting*, Methodist Publishing House, 1998, pp. 4–11, and Volume 2, *Growing into Hope: Liberation and Change*, Methodist Publishing House, 1998, pp. 4–13.

25 Reddie, *Growing into Hope: Liberation and Change*, pp. 8–10.

26 For a wider discussion on this issue, see Emmanuel Lartey, *In Living Colour: An Intercultural Approach to Pastoral Care and Counselling*, Cassells, 1997.

27 James Michael Lee, *The Content of Religious Instruction*, Religious Education Press, 1985, p. 257.

28 James M. Jones, *Educating Black People for Liberation and Creative Growth*, The United Church Press, 1970, pp. 7–14, and M. Lee Montgomery, *The Education of Black Children: What Black Educators Are Saying*, The Hawthorn Press, Inc., 1970, pp. 49–50.

29 James Baldwin, *Nobody Knows My Name*, Corgi, 1965, p. 121.

30 Baldwin, *Nobody Knows My Name*, p. 121.

31 Mairtin Mac an Ghaill, 'Young, Gifted and Black: Methodological Reflections of a Teacher/Researcher', in Geoffrey Walford, *Doing Educational Research*, The Open University, 1991, p. 101.

32 W.E.B. Dubois, *The Souls of Black Folk*, Bantam Books, 1989, p. 3.

33 Reddie, *Faith, Stories and the Experience of Black Elders: Singing the Lord's Song in a Strange Land*, Jessica Kingsley, 2001, pp. 32–34.

34 Reddie, *Faith, Stories and the Experience of Black Elders*, pp. 36–38.

35 See James Fowler, *Stages of Faith*, Harper, 1986.

36 Reddie, *Faith, Stories and the Experience of Black Elders*, pp. 47–53.

37 Reddie, *Faith, Stories and the Experience of Black Elders*, pp. 54–61.

38 Reddie, *Faith, Stories and the Experience of Black Elders*, pp. 116–20.

39 See Lartey, *In Living Colour*, pp. 85–111.

40 See Acts 17:16–32.

41 See Stephen B. Bevans, *Models of Contextual Theology*, Orbis, 1992.

42 Reddie, *Growing into Hope: Believing and Expecting*, pp. 3–10.

43 Reddie, *Nobodies to Somebodies: A Practical Theology for Education and Liberation*, Epworth, 2003.

44 Paulo Freire, 'Education, Liberation and the Church', in Jeff Francis Astley, Leslie J. Astley and Colin Crowder (eds.), *Theological Perspectives on Christian Formation: A Reader on Theology and Christian Education*, Gracewing and Eerdmans, 1996, p. 169.

45 See Grant S. Shockley, 'Black Theology and Religious Education', in Randolph Crump Miller (ed.), *Theologies of Religious Education*, Religious Education Press, 1995.

46 See Beckford, *Dread and Pentecostal*.

47 See Beckford, *Jesus is Dread*.

48 Reddie, *Faith, Stories and the Experience of Black Elders*, pp. 90–94.

49 Reddie, 'Keeping it Real', in *The Fruits of the Spirit: The 2002 Christian*, Foundery Press, 2002, pp. 164–68.

50 Jamaican Creole or Patois is a cultural synthesis of traditional African religions and English, originating in the Caribbean in the 18th and 19th centuries when African slaves were transplanted from Africa to other parts of the world. See Emile L. Adams, *Understanding Jamaican Patois*, Kingston Publishers Ltd, 1991, and Carol Tomlin, *Black Language Style in Sacred and Secular Contexts*, Caribbean Diaspora Press, 1999.

51 Tomlin, *Black Language Style in Sacred and Secular Contexts*.

52   Janice Hale (Benson), *Black Children: Their Roots, Culture and Learning Styles*, The Johns Hopkins University Press, 1986, pp. 21–44.

53   Lerleen Willis, 'All Things to All Men? Or What has Language to Do with Gender and Resistance in the Black Majority Churches in Britain?', in *Black Theology In Britain: A Journal of Contextual Praxis*, Vol. 4, No. 2, Sheffield Academic Press, 2002.

54   Jillian Brown (selected essay and poems), in Anthony G. Reddie, *Legacy: Anthology in Memory of Jillian Brown*, Methodist Publishing House, 2000, pp. 33–38.

55   Lorraine Dixon, 'bell hooks: Teller of truth and dreamer of dreams', in Reddie, *Legacy*, pp. 129–137.

56   Jacquelyn Grant, *White Women's Christ, and Black Women's Jesus*, Scholars Press, 1989.

57   See Sewell, *Black Masculinities and Schooling*.

58   See Beckford, *Dread and Pentecostal*, pp. 165–66.

59   See Michael Eric Dyson, *Reflecting Black: African American Cultural Criticism*, University of Minnesota Press, 1993, and Michael Eric Dyson, *Between God and Gangsta Rap: Bearing Witness to Black Culture*, Oxford University Press, 1996.

Deep currents of the heart

60   Mike Riddell, *The Insatiable Moon*, HarperCollins New Zealand, 1997.

Ritual as strategic practice

61   An alternative worship community in Ealing, London. See www.freshworship.org.

62   Fiona Bowie, *The Anthropology of Religion*, Blackwell, 2000, p. 151.

63   Robert Bocock, *Ritual in Industrial Society*, Allen and Unwin, 1974, p. 30.

64   Bobby C. Alexander, 'Ritual and Current Studies of Ritual: Overview', in Stephen D. Glazier, *Anthropology of Religion: A Handbook*, Praeger, 1997, p. 141.

65   Ronald Grimes, *Ritual Criticism: Case Studies in Practice, Essays on its Theory*, University of South Carolina Press, 1990, p. 135.

66   Bani Shorter, *Susceptible to the Sacred: The Psychological Experience of Ritual*, Routledge, 1996, p. 121.

67   Catherine Bell, *Ritual Theory, Ritual Practice*, Oxford University Press, 1992.

68   Pierre Bourdieu, *Outline of a Theory of Practice*, Cambridge University Press, 1977. He uses the term 'habitus' to refer to the unconscious dispositions, the classificatory systems and taken-for-granted preferences that an individual has, which operate at the level of everyday knowledge and are inscribed on to the individual's body, that is, they are part of who they are as persons. The insight that this gives is 'to confront the act itself' by addressing the 'socially informed body' with all its senses. The body is the factor that unifies all practice. Bourdieu writes that these senses include 'the traditional five senses... But also the sense of necessity, and the sense of duty, the sense of direction and the sense of reality, the sense of balance and the sense of beauty, common sense and the sense of the sacred, tactical sense and the sense of responsibility, business sense and the sense of propriety, the sense of humour and the sense of absurdity, moral sense and the sense of practicality, and so on' (p. 104). Bell adds that a 'sense of ritual' would be a vital addition to the list in most cultures.

69   I part company with Bell in her third one (misrecognition), which seems to me to be an incredibly patronizing notion. I agree with De Certeau who dismisses it in Bordieu's work: 'With these "strategies"... knowledgeable but unknown, the most traditionalist ethnology returns... Today an ethnologist would no longer dare to say that. How can Bourdieu compromise himself thus in the name of sociology?' (Michel De Certeau, *The Practice of Everyday Life*, University of California Press, 1984, p. 56).

70   See, for example, Peter Brierley, *The Tide Is Running Out*, Christian Research, 2000.

71   John Drane, *Cultural Change and Biblical Faith*, Paternoster, 2000.

72   T.J. Scheff, *Catharsis in Healing Ritual and Drama*, University of California Press, 1979, p. 120. Scheff argues that one of the functions of good ritual is to create appropriate distance for people to express emotions. Overdistancing leaves no room for expressing emotions.

73 The combination of consumption and communication and information technologies and its effect on religious practice is explored in detail in David Lyon, *Jesus in Disneyland: Religion in Postmodern Times*, Polity Press, 2000.

74 Zygmunt Bauman, *Life in Fragments*, Blackwell, 1995, p. 89.

75 Lyon, *Jesus in Disneyland*.

76 Alan Jamieson, *A Churchless Faith*, SPCK, 2002.

77 Catherine Bell, *Ritual: Perspectives and Dimensions*, Oxford University Press, 1997, p. 81.

78 The Labyrinth referred to here is the one originally installed at St Pauls Cathedral, which incorporates various stations en route. See www.labyrinth.org.uk for details.

79 Redemptive hegemony is a synthesis of Burridge's notion of 'redemptive process' and Gramsci's notion of hegemony, cited in Bell, *Ritual Theory, Ritual Practice*, p. 83.

80 Some of these reflections on reforming tradition are inspired by Tom Beaudoin in his book *Virtual Faith*, Jossey Bass, 1998.

81 Victor Turner, *The Ritual Process: Structure and Anti Structure*, Routledge, 1969.

82 Sally Moore and Barbara Myerhoff, cited in Bell, *Ritual Theory, Ritual Practice*, p. 123.

83 David Bosch, *Transforming Mission*, Orbis Books, 1991.

REFRESHING WORSHIP

BRIAN & KEVIN DRAPER

Many people involved in church life are on the lookout for ways of keeping weekly worship fresh and vital. Over the last few years, several groups have pioneered inventive new services and way of doing and being church, with the aim of creating truly authentic worshipping communities. Brian and Kevin Draper, who helped dream one such service into life, ask what we can learn from our experience of church worship, whether it is in new or traditional settings. They consider the theoretical and practical implications of revitalising worship for people of all ages and, throughout the book, they provide many examples of how, in very simple ways, we can all start to make a difference. With fresh vision and resources, we can inspire not only those with whom we worship regularly, but even those outside the church altogether.

ISBN 1 84101 146 0   £5.99
To order, please turn to page 109.

A PREACHER'S COMPANION

ESSAYS FROM THE COLLEGE OF PREACHERS
EDITED BY STEPHEN WRIGHT, GEOFFREY HUNTER & GETHIN THOMAS

This book is a practical collection of articles from the College of Preachers for everybody involved in preaching, regularly or occasionally. Designed to stimulate thought and provide guidance for practice, it presents encouragement, fresh ideas and suggestions for further reflection and study, and draws helpful insights from the fields of cultural and communication research, as well as theology and biblical teaching. Included are contributions from Lavinia Byrne, Donald Coggan, David Day, Douglas Cleverley Ford, Colin Morris, Lesslie Newbigin, Susan Sayers and Michael Turnbull.

Founded in 1960 under the guidance of Donald Coggan, later to become Archbishop of Canterbury, the College of Preachers fosters excellence in preaching in all mainstream Christian churches, aiming to be biblical, thoughtful, practical, ecumenical and radical. Based at Spurgeon's College, south London, the College runs a range of training courses, and publishes a Journal in which many of the articles in this volume first appeared.

ISBN 1 84101 254 8   £9.99
To order, please turn to page 109.

CLOWNS, STORYTELLERS, DISCIPLES

SPIRITUALITY AND CREATIVITY FOR TODAY'S CHURCH
OLIVE M. FLEMING DRANE

The call to be culturally relevant while also remaining biblically rooted is arguably the greatest challenge facing today's Christians. Olive Fleming Drane addresses this question in a unique style as she combines the story of her own spiritual journey with informed theological reflection on the bigger picture of what God is doing in today's world.

As she recounts her pilgrimage from personal tragedy to international ministry in the creative arts, she not only offers an inspirational account of God at work, but also provides plenty of practical suggestions for innovative ministry. There are specific ideas for interactive Bible study, as well as clear guidance on how churches and individuals might begin to use the arts with theological integrity—offering a unique resource for the renewal of worship and evangelism in a postmodern world.

ISBN 1 84101 226 2   £7.99
To order, please turn to page 109.

GROWING LEADERS

REFLECTIONS ON LEADERSHIP, LIFE AND JESUS
JAMES LAWRENCE

Seven out of ten Christian leaders feel overworked, four in ten suffer financial pressure, only two in ten have had management training, and 1500 give up their job over a ten-year period. At the same time, as financial restrictions affect the availability of full-time ministers, more people are needed for leadership roles in local congregations, for every area of church work.

This book faces the challenge of raising up new leaders and helping existing leaders to mature, using the model for growing leaders at the heart of the Arrow Leadership Programme, a ministry of the Church Pastoral Aid Society (CPAS). It comprehensively surveys leadership skills and styles, discerning our personal calling, avoiding the 'red zone' of stress, developing character, and living as part of the community of God's people.

ISBN 1 84101 246 7   £8.99
To order, please turn to page 109.

PRAYING THE JESUS PRAYER TOGETHER

BROTHER RAMON & SIMON BARRINGTON-WARD

The Jesus Prayer is an ancient yet simple form of contemplative prayer, rooted in scripture. Over the last few decades it has spread out of the Eastern Orthodox tradition and into the lives and spirituality of Western Christians, causing a quiet revolution.

Both Brother Ramon (the hermit) and Simon Barrington-Ward (the bishop) had been practising and teaching the Jesus Prayer for well over twenty years when they came together for a shared week of prayer at Glasshampton Monastery. This book shares what they learned in an experience they described as a 'week of glory', yet also marked by the physical suffering of Brother Ramon's final illness.

ISBN 1 84101 147 9   £6.99
To order, please turn to page 109.

ORDER FORM

REF	TITLE	PRICE	QTY	TOTAL
146 0	*Refreshing Worship*	£5.99		
254 8	*A Preacher's Companion*	£9.99		
226 2	*Clowns, Storytellers, Disciples*	£7.99		
246 7	*Growing Leaders*	£8.99		
147 9	*Praying the Jesus Prayer Together*	£6.99		

POSTAGE AND PACKING CHARGES						
order value	UK	Europe	Surface	Air Mail	Postage and packing:	
£7.00 & under	£1.25	£3.00	£3.50	£5.50	Donation:	
£7.01–£30.00	£2.25	£5.50	£6.50	£10.00	**Total enclosed:**	
Over £30.00	free	prices on request				

Name _____ Account Number _____

Address_____

_____ Postcode _____

Telephone Number _____ Email _____

Payment by: Cheque ❑ Mastercard ❑ Visa ❑ Postal Order ❑ Switch ❑

Credit card no. ❑❑❑❑ ❑❑❑❑ ❑❑❑❑ ❑❑❑❑   Expires ❑❑ ❑❑

Switch card no. ❑❑❑❑❑❑❑❑❑❑❑❑❑❑❑❑❑❑

Issue no. of Switch card ❑❑❑❑   Expires ❑❑ ❑❑

Signature _____ Date _____

All orders must be accompanied by the appropriate payment.

Please send your completed order form to:
BRF, First Floor, Elsfield Hall, 15–17 Elsfield Way, Oxford OX2 8FG
Tel. 01865 319700 / Fax. 01865 319701 Email: enquiries@brf.org.uk

❑ Please send me further information about BRF publications.

Available from your local Christian bookshop.   BRF is a Registered Charity